A CASSANDRA AT WESTMINSTER

DONALD McI. JOHNSON

A

CASSANDRA

AT

WESTMINSTER

JOHNSON

LONDON

DONALD McI. JOHNSON © 1967

First published 1967

SET IN 11/12 POINT BASKERVILLE AND PRINTED AND MADE IN GREAT
BRITAIN BY MORRISON AND GIBB LTD., LONDON AND EDINBURGH,
FOR JOHNSON PUBLICATIONS LTD., 11/14 STANHOPE MEWS WEST,
LONDON, S.W.7

CONTENTS

CONTENTS

ACKNOWLEDGMENTS

are due first to those who shared these adventures in the political sphere of which I write, particularly to Betty and the family, who have been at my side and supported me wholeheartedly throughout; to those who have encouraged and assisted me in the writing of this book; and to those who have unwittingly contributed to its pages and in so many instances have given me permission to use their quotations. In making acknowledgments in advance to my future readers I have to apologise for the fact that this book does not contain illustrations, but one of the principal effects of thirty years in public life is to make one allergic to the sight of one's own face in print.

D. McI. J.

INTRODUCTION

THIS book is written as a personal documentary in the same manner as have been my previous books in a series of autobiographies.

In my capacity as a chronicler of the times, I have in the present instance had the additional fortune to be a close witness of, even a minor participator in, events of historical importance. My story is woven round a sorry catalogue of disaster—the decline and fall of Mr. Harold Macmillan, the decline and fall of the Conservative Party, the decline of the House of Commons at Westminster, the social decay of the British nation—against which I did my utmost to give warning within the limitations of my position and abilities. Moreover, since these baleful happenings reached a climacteric in the Profumo affair, and since that was the juncture at which I became personally involved to a maximum extent, much of what I have to say pivots on this.

It will undoubtedly be one criticism that I am 'digging up events best forgotten' and that 'we must look to the future'. But how can we study with any benefit the problems that confront us in the future unless we analyse the past and so endeavour to understand their origin? The simultaneous decay both of the Conservative cause and of representative parliamentary democracy, so closely interconnected with each other, pose problems of a complexity that are incapable of solution without such analysis being made.

Our present time resembles in many ways that of the Renaissance. A stable society with its rigid class system is dissolving before our eyes: fixed principles of conduct in the behaviour of man towards man are being thrown overboard. It resembles too that of the decline of the Roman Empire—the winds of change which howl about our ears already blow the waters of the Orontes into the Tiber. It is a time, above all, in which men and women are becoming increasingly uncertain as to the nature of the society in which they live.

It may be that, at some future date, the present time will be looked upon with similar regard to that given to the Renaissance era with the breaking out of the human spirit, bound in rigid fashion for so long, into new forms of artistic production and fresh scientific discovery: and it would be wrong for anyone of older years not to appreciate this.

But politics, rather than art and science, are the theme of this book and it would be equally wrong not to express concern at the trends which one has seen at such close hand during almost a decade in Parliament. For, whatever form our society may take when it 'gels' once more, the only adjectives that can describe it at the moment are of a pejorative nature.

Not Gladstone, nor Disraeli, not even Keir Hardie nor Karl Marx, is the patron political saint of to-day, but rather is it Machiavelli who occupies this important niche. We live in a non-ethical, conspiratorial society in which the main canon of political behaviour is for men to combine in secret to conspire against each other and the remainder of society.

Such conspiracies are familiar to us as Committees, those bodies in which men can intrigue under the most respectable of auspices, beneath the specious guise of benevolent invention, under conditions of secrecy to which they are so passionately devoted. Above and beyond the Committee is the gigantic conspiracy of the bureaucracy which dominates the State under its own shroud of secret process, of which only an occasional small corner is lifted even by the most sensational of 'exposures'.

A society of this nature is no longer governed by law or by sound principles of good government, but by Committee resolutions—resolutions which at their best are founded on expediency, at their worst originate in emotion, or even malice. The most powerful and influential figure amongst us is the Chairman of the Committee: to him all bow down in his omnipotence. Conversely, you are nobody to-day if you are not the Chairman of a Committee.

The natural enemy of this society is the individual who acts openly and guides his actions on principle, while refusing to bind himself to any of the Establishments who claim as of right to regard him as their creature. Such a man is a marked man—one to be hunted down and utterly destroyed by any means available. Against him the entire conspiratorial society, severally and collectively, acts in unison.

The traditional bastions of a liberal society still exist. But they do so in crumbling condition.

Parliament still sits in public with procedures which, to a limited extent, protect the individual operator. But, as an assembly based on personal independence, it has perished inasmuch as it is completely controlled by the two large Party machines which prefer to conduct their affairs in secret and conspiratorial fashion and whose pressures over recent times have had the effect of making open debates increasingly a sham.

The Courts of Law still retain their sturdy tradition of fairness and independence in the protection of the individual. But here too their powers are being eroded by bureaucratic legislation: more and more they become 'the handmaidens of the administration'.

It is against this background that the struggles of an individual, of which I now have to tell, have taken place. It is not surprising perhaps that I came to clash with that most Machiavellian politician of modern times, Mr. Harold Macmillan. In one contemporary *Daily Telegraph* commentary at the time of the Profumo crisis, I was referred to as 'a modern Cato': rather would I prefer to be considered 'a modern Brutus'.

Until I had conjured up my present title for this book, it had been my intention to christen this book 'The Great Sickness of the Conservative Party'. For it is a sombre comment that the 'conspiracies', amongst whom I must include the two large political Parties, and who are so adept at stigmatizing an opponent—clearly I shall already be regarded as self-condemned as a 'paranoiac'—are prone themselves to nervous breakdown within their closed societies and it is one such that forms the central theme of my story.

In conclusion, not being in any professional relationship to Mr. Harold Macmillan, I have felt at liberty to comment on his state of health prior to his operation in October 1963, and during the final months of his Prime Ministership. The fate of nations, certainly the fate of the Conservative Party, depended during those years on the level of Mr. Macmillan's blood urea: it is accordingly a matter of historic interest that it should be discussed. I am hoping that the comments of an experienced doctor will be of value. Though perhaps this will be considered an additional reason why any such doctor is a potential menace in the House of Commons.

CHAPTER ONE

AN UNUSUAL EVENT

Out flew the web and floated wide
The mirror cracked from side to side
'The curse is come upon me' cried
The Lady of Shalott.

WHETHER a book moves steadily forward from its first page, as do the autobiographies of my publishing firm's elderly medical authors who (as we always insist) start with their childhood days and proceed from there, or whether it moves backwards in the manner of Thornton Wilder's *The Bridge of San Luis Rey*, there is inevitably some finite point of time at which it must begin.

This book begins therefore at 10.57 a.m. precisely on Friday morning, 22nd March 1963, when, having handed my hat and umbrella to one of our assiduous attendants in the Members' Cloakroom of the House of Commons, I turned idly towards the news tape, already cut into its first lengths and displayed on the board.

As any of my former colleagues must confirm, for an M.P. to be in attendance at 10.57 a.m. on a Friday morning—which is, of course, the day for Private Members' Bills and Motions when attendance is entirely voluntary—must betoken either an exceptional interest in the day's events or, alternatively, an exceptional state of mental aberration. In my case it must have been the latter. For I cannot remember for what reason I was there on this particular day. The fact that I was there at all must be numbered amongst the unusual coincidences which bespatter the pages of this book.

For what I read upon the tape was the first surprising

indication that at 11 a.m. that morning—in three minutes' time, in fact—The Right Hon. John Profumo, Secretary of State for War, was proposing to make a personal statement to the House of Commons.

My steps quickened as I mounted the stone steps of the balustraded staircase leading to the Principal Floor and the Debating Chamber. This was it! Would he get away with it, or wouldn't he? The name, Profumo, and its association with this simple question had, over the past three to four weeks, been the sole topic of 'behind the scenes' conversation in all the nooks and crannies of this Westminster edifice in which such matters are apt to form the topic of conversation. The House in general, the Party in particular, was on edge. The Macmillan decay had set in: the spy scandals, the Vassall Tribunal, the ministerial resignations—not to mention the Argyll divorce case as an independent operation. All this— and Profumo too! It was, as my friend, Harry Kerby,* liked to say, 'doing the boys no good'. The Kissing Ring was shaken. Definitely shaken.

The rumours that had started almost immediately after the shooting incident at 17 Wimpole Mews on 14th December 1962, had continued to fester. There had been first Profumo and Christine Keeler: and the Russian agent, Ivanov. Then the appearance in the public eye of the sinister figure of Stephen Ward—'Dr.' Stephen Ward, as he was universally referred to. From there they had escalated. Unmentionable incidents were connected with unmentionable names. Finally, there came the climax with the 'missing witness' episode, as the psychopathic temperament of the girl witness, so closely concerned with the trial of Johnnie Edgcombe, had led to her melodramatic dash to Spain—with, of course, the opposite effect to that which was originally intended.

But they would be able to hush it up! THEY had hushed up things before, and THEY would hush things up again. Moreover, ministers had had mistresses before, and would have them again. One needn't go back to Charles James Fox:

* Captain Henry Kerby, Conservative M.P. for Arundel and Shoreham Division of Sussex.

there had been, in more recent times, the venerable figure of David Lloyd George and nobody, or nobody amongst the general public anyway, had known of his scandalous way of life. What was the angle on this thing, anyway? This might be the century of the common man, but, none the less, up until that time the fierce searchlights of Fleet Street had seemed to lose their powers of penetration in the protective smoke screen that surrounded those in certain levels of society.

Undoubtedly, even in his worst nightmares, John Profumo himself could not have dreamed that his casual note, so indiscreetly written on War Office paper, would ultimately find itself displayed in the popular Press after, incidentally, leading to his own ruin and the political scandal of the century.

Then, too, there was the strange behaviour of the *Sunday Pictorial*. No less an authority than Lord Denning in his Report confirms that Christine Keeler, in the course of marshalling her assets in the plight in which she had found herself, had sold her letter to the *Sunday Pictorial* and that the *Sunday Pictorial*, despite the proud 'publish and be damned' boast of its journalistic stable, having bought the document for £1000 in January, had stood about for some time shifting this hot potato from one hand to the other, and had finally put it in the safe, where, at the time of the action which I have so far described, it remained.

However, practically everyone about the place—that is everyone with the possible exception of Mr. Harold Macmillan —knew about the letter in the safe at the *Sunday Pictorial*.

I have to admit that, when I was first told of the letter by Harry Kerby as he sat, like some latter-day Merlin, in the centre of his vast web of intrigue in Interview Room 12, House of Commons, I considered this one of Harry's most unlikely rumours—rumours which, however, I have usually found come true in the end. Indeed, it might have remained in the sphere of rumour. But the papers were edging forward inch by inch: and Profumo was unlucky.

He was unlucky in that the two journalists, Messrs. Foster and Mulholland, had only recently been sent to prison in connection with their refusal to divulge sources of evidence to the Vassall Tribunal: and this made their colleagues perhaps more dedicated than usual in their legitimate task of clarifying what must have seemed to them a parallel case.

Moreover, Heaven did not save him from his blundering friends. It must have appeared a bright idea to Stephen Ward and to Mr. Paul Mann to get Christine Keeler out of the country before she had to face the ordeal of being a material witness at the Johnnie Edgcombe trial on Thursday, 14th March. But, of course, it was not.

For on Sunday, the 17th, the *Sunday Pictorial*, having scrapped the Keeler story, published a Stephen Ward story instead; while the *News of the World*, not to be outdone, had come out with 'The Two Worlds of Christine Keeler' by Peter Earle.

'In the world of high society', wrote Peter Earle, 'Christine was guided by her friend, Stephen Ward.

'His many friends were aware of the interest and philanthropic patience and helpfulness which he showed towards the girls, many of whom were comparatively unknown and of humble origins.

'They also remembered how well many of the girls had done in later life, entirely through the guidance of this handsome scholarly bachelor.'

This had been the first that I personally had heard of Stephen Ward, though I was subsequently to find that his name, in his professional capacity as an osteopath, was well known amongst my parliamentary colleagues. It did not seem to me to take more than an ordinary degree of worldly experience to sum him up as far as his leisure activities were concerned.

Then also, during the preceding week, there had been the famous issue of the *Daily Express* of Friday, 15th March. 'WAR MINISTER SHOCK' runs the headline of the page which I still possess and have in front of me as I write. Beneath the headline is the story by Ian Aitken: 'Mr. John Profumo, the War Minister, has offered his resignation to Mr. Macmillan for personal reasons. The Prime Minister has asked him to stay on. There has been speculation about Mr. Profumo's future among M.P.s for several weeks.' Adjacent to this in the next column is the 5 in. by 3½ in. photograph of Mr. John Profumo and his wife, formerly Miss Valerie Hobson. In the middle column is an advertisement trailer for future *Express* features, 'NEXT WEEK: Who's the girl at your side this spring?' Further over to the right again is the headline 'OLD BAILEY WITNESS' and the 7 in. by 5½ in. photograph, the caption of which still has to inform us that 'This is Christine Keeler'. All this, as the *Daily Express* subsequently explained to Lord Denning, was by accidental juxtaposition. Perhaps this was so: perhaps it was that the same element of precognition and coincidence that will occur from time to time throughout this story was responsible for the fact that these striking photographs found themselves all together on the front page: but it had only one message for those who had been hearing the rumours.

Finally, there was Andie Roth and his *Westminster Confidential*. All the gunpowder that had accumulated in the underground passages and along the lobbies of the House of Commons needed only a spark to ignite it and that spark was provided by Andie Roth, the slightly mysterious American who specialises in publishing particulars of the business background of M.P.s and other such interesting literature, and whose *Westminster Confidential* at that time circulated round some hundreds of people, including, of course, Members of Parliament themselves. *Westminster Confidential* of 8th March had had this about 'the girls':

'One of the choicest bits in their stories was a letter, apparently signed "J———" on the stationery of the Secretary of War. The allegation by this girl was that not only was this Minister, who has a famous actress wife, her friend, but also the Soviet Military Attaché, apparently a Colonel Ivanov. The famous actress wife, of course, would sue for divorce, the scandal ran. Who was using the girl to "milk" whom of information—the War Secretary or the Soviet Military Attaché—ran the minds of those primarily interested in security.'

It took time for *Westminster Confidential* to percolate. But percolate it did, while the most eminent legal brains in the country were paralysed, not knowing what to do in the face of this small elusive paper with its equally elusive editor.

All this created the atmosphere without which the subsequent parliamentary events, so well detailed by Lord Denning in his Report, could not have taken place. Quite apart from Mr. George Wigg's and Mrs. Barbara Castle's questions late at night on Thursday, 21st March, it had reached the stage when, on that same day, during the consideration of so mundane a matter as an enactment relating to sewage and drainage in connection with the London Government Bill which was passing through Standing Committee, Mr. Ben Parkin, Labour M.P. for North Paddington, asked if this part of the Bill had been considered in detail at Cabinet level:

'We hear a lot of chit-chat,' said Mr. Parkin. 'There's the case of the missing model, where we understand there's a system whereby a model can be easily obtained for the convenience of a Minister of the Crown.'

Sir Samuel Storey, Chairman of the Committee, rightly asked what this had to do with sewage and is reputed to have been genuinely mystified. But he was one of a minority.

By this time, indeed, the lion had eaten Young Albert and somebody 'had to be summonsed'.

Lord Denning has set down in words far more cogent than any at my disposal the detail of the meeting of the Famous Five—Chief Whip (Mr. Martin Redmayne), Leader of the House (Mr. Iain Macleod), Minister without Portfolio (Mr. William Deedes), Attorney General (Sir John Hobson), Solicitor General (Sir Peter Rawlinson)—which took place between 3 a.m. and 4 a.m. on the morning of 22nd March and their interview with Mr. John Profumo at that extraordinary time. ('I am sure that, had we had time . . .' said Miss Valerie Hobson later to Lord Denning, implying that they might have done better. And she was, of course, right.)

But on that Friday, as I took my seat in the Chamber next to my colleague, Norman Pannell,* I was totally unaware of this meeting and so doubtless were the majority of the small

* Norman Pannell, Conservative M.P. for Kirkdale Division of Liverpool.

gathering of M.P.s present. There was an unusual array of
top brass on the Front Bench for a Friday morning—the
Prime Minister (Mr. Harold Macmillan), the Chief Whip, the
Leader of the House and, in addition, Mr. John Profumo
making his famous statement:

'My friend, Miss Keeler . . . our standing invitation to visit
Dr. Stephen Ward . . . Mr. Ivanov, whom we met at a house
party . . .'

But:

'There was no impropriety whatsoever in my acquaintance-
ship with Miss Keeler . . . I shall not hesitate to issue writs
for libel and slander if scandalous allegations are made or
repeated outside the House.'

It was of the stuff of phantasy. The sex connotation which
was the extraordinary part of this statement—and which was
subsequently to cause dismay and mystification amongst our
friends and other observers, particularly those on the continent
of Europe—seemed quite redundant. (Why, ran the logical
Continental mind, should not a Minister have a girl, or even
a mistress? What is there so out of the way about that?) The
only public charge from which John Profumo had to defend
himself was that of causing the disappearance of a witness
and the consequent perversion of justice—something of which
nobody seriously suspected him to be guilty anyway. Why did
his sex life have to come out in this stupid fashion and be
displayed with consequences that brought the entire British
nation into derision? This is the first of many unanswered
questions.

For, quite apart from the exact state of his virtue, here
was this golden boy of the Establishment gratuitously advertising in a statement of nation-wide interest the disreputable
company with whom he had been associating.

Here too was the Prime Minister giving this favourite of
his choice a pat on the back before he sat down. To be fair
to him, Mr. Macmillan could probably not have read the
News of the World item by Peter Earle on the previous Sunday,
which is perhaps natural, as the *News of the World* did not
seem to have printed this item in all its editions.

According to later Press accounts there were the cheers from the Tory backbenchers. Though they were certainly not very loud cheers. Indeed there were two backbenchers—Norman Pannell and myself, sitting in our usual seats on the second bench below the gangway—from whom there were no cheers at all, but merely a quick exchange, *sotto voce*, of which you will find no record in Hansard.

'I suppose the girl's a * * *,' said Norman Pannell.

'And Ward a * * *,' I added.

It is only proper that the unparliamentary words we used should be represented by old-fashioned asterisks.

Certainly no occasion for cheering! How now of 'the Party image'?

I was not myself in any mood for cheering. At the end of a busy parliamentary week, the Party image was at that moment of time no mere insubstantial wraith as far as I was concerned. With the fourth year of Parliament half-way through, the firmament was resounding with ideas to burnish up the Party image. Such ideas, as often as not, involve the co-operation of the Member of Parliament in his own constituency and, earlier in the year, one of the Conservative Central Office gremlins had thought up the best idea so far. This was that every M.P. should write a personal letter to all the B List voters (new arrivals) in his constituency, extending his welcome to them and explaining the welfare service that he was able to offer.

As far as I was concerned in Carlisle, there were some 6000 voters on the B List. An anonymous benefactor had provided the amount of postage, but I was to provide the House of Commons paper (at the ultimate out-of-pocket cost to me of £6 10s.) and, of course, I was to sign the letters. 'They would look so much better with the Member's own signature.' On that Friday morning the 6000 letters to B List voters in Carlisle were all waiting at home for my signature. The roughest of calculations will show this to be a full week-end's work.

'Rubbing up the handle of the big front door' as a form of political apprenticeship just wasn't in it! (Though was I ever to be 'the ruler of the Queen's Navee'? I had begun to doubt it.)

The image of the Conservative Party! Each signature of mine, with the corresponding loss of leisure which it involved, was merely a drop of water endeavouring to fill up a leaky bucket in the circumstances that had arisen.

Feelings of irritation and revolt were an instinctive reaction.

Who am I to say that I considered Mr. John Profumo a liar? I merely felt a strange certainty that this was not to be the last that we would hear of him.

Before starting to append my 6000 signatures to B List voters that evening, I sat down and wrote two other letters. One was to the Chairman of my constituency Association to say that, with the Profumo statement, I felt 'the Party leadership had lost its moral authority'. With the Council Elections coming on I did not want to bother him just now, but in due course I would want to discuss my position with him and the other Officers. The other one was in a similar vein to the Chief Whip.

I then went on dutifully to sign my letters to the B List voters. Though, in the light of subsequent events, I might as well have thrown them all into the fire.

CHAPTER TWO

GINGER AT A DISCOUNT

IN THESE days 'Ginger Groups' are perennially in the news. Once upon a time, and it is so long ago that I have some difficulty in reminding myself of it, I was the Chairman of a Ginger Group myself. If you do not know this about me, it is scarcely your fault, as this was long before the days when young Chairmen of Ginger Groups were rushed in front of the TV cameras to achieve instant nation-wide renown. I did not even get a mention on the steam radio—nor yet, as far as I can remember, in the National Press.

None the less, following the Liberal Party Assembly of 1941, at which I had made more row than most of those present at the generally stagnant state of the Liberal Party at that time, and, in particular, the irksome and disadvantageous nature of the wartime Party Truce, I found myself, following a private indignation meeting, the Chairman of the *soi-disant* Liberal Action Group. (Later to become known as 'Radical Action'.) Its purpose was to give the apparently moribund Liberal Party 'a modern image'. (Though in those days a different term was used.)

The Liberal Action Group can make justifiable claim to be amongst the first of many such groups of younger politicians which have blossomed with varying degrees of success and public acclaim over the past twenty-five years. In its way— just as Richard Acland's Commonwealth Party, with its glamorous young Forces' candidates winning wartime by-elections, produced the prototype of the glamorous youthful Parliamentary candidates of to-day—it was the forerunner of such more politically newsworthy and successful groups as the 'One Nation' group or even (one says it with bated breath) the Bow Group. But the Liberal Action Group had virtually no publicity at all. In the current state of the 'black' that, for a variety of reasons, was on the Liberal Party in those days throughout most of the British national Press, it caused little more sensation than if it had been a local group for parish council reform.

However, it struggled on in obscurity and under difficulties of wartime communication, exchanging memoranda, holding conferences, making pronouncements. These naturally were 'radical' pronouncements of a content probably neither better nor worse than those of its successors. In the end it did nothing that mattered and led nowhere. (Apart from anything else, these were still the days when young, even comparatively young, people in politics were expected to be seen and not heard and to await their turn before they spoke.) But at least it was a national Group and that its members were of national political calibre is brought back to me from time to time when I reflect on such names as those of George Grey (talented young Liberal M.P. for Berwick, killed in so untimely a fashion in the Normandy landings in 1944), Mark Bonham Carter, Donald Wade (former Liberal Party Chief Whip in Parliament and now Lord Wade), Margot Naylor (now investment columnist of *The Observer*), Honor Balfour (now London Correspondent of *Time and Life*) and consider how both they and others of equal ability, but not quite so fortunate in making a break-through in public life, might have fared had we had a little more good fortune at our beck and call.

For it is not quite true that the Liberal Action Group led nowhere. It led me to the Chippenham by-election of August 1943, at which, fighting as an Independent candidate, I lost by merely 195 votes. Then to a participation in the Darwen by-election of November of the same year, when Honor Balfour lost by 70 votes. These were two near misses for the Liberal cause within six months of each other which, had they come out of the bag the other way, might well have changed political history. ('It was always the Tories who had

the luck,' we used to say in the Liberal Party in those days.)
But these are described in detail in my book, *Bars and Barricades*, as also are my diverting, but unsuccessful election-eering efforts elsewhere, in which I am able to include that ultimate accolade for any senior politician of to-day—a share in the campaign against Mr. Quintin Hogg in the Oxford 'Munich' by-election of October 1938, at which under the stress of events the normal alignments of British politics became temporarily more blurred than at any other time during the past twenty-five years. Participating as a Liberal, I found myself working within a broad political spectrum of Communists, Labour Party (including two members of future Labour Governments, Richard Crossman and Frank Pakenham) and dissident anti-Chamberlain Conservatives. Amongst these latter was an Independent Conservative M.P. who felt so strongly on the current issues that he came down to Oxford to speak against his own Party candidate. The name —Harold Macmillan. Amongst my co-workers also, although I did not know this until a much later date, was an under-graduate plying to and fro on a bicycle, Edward Heath.

However, at the end of the day, my failure with the Liberal Action Group was a dismal one. The Group passed into other hands. While at the General Election of 1945 in the Chippen-ham Division I suffered my fourth Election defeat in ten years as a Liberal Parliamentary Candidate. My subsequent feelings of disappointment at the hopelessness of the Liberals led to my resignation from the Liberal Party and, in the immediate post-war years, I found myself in the political wilderness.

But the political wilderness was not entirely an unfriendly place. I had made a minor political reputation for myself at the Chippenham by-election in 1943 and, for the only occasion that I can remember, I was the object of almost flattering attention from those with more famous names than my own. David Eccles,* my successful Conservative opponent at Chippenham, was indicating to me that I would

---

* Subsequently the Right Hon. Viscount Eccles, Minister of Works, Minister of Education, member of Mr. Harold Macmillan's Cabinet until July 1963.

be welcome in the Conservative Party: Frank Pakenham*
my Oxford acquaintance, was making similar hints as regards
the Labour Party.

After months of agonising reappraisal, I decided to join
the Conservative Party.

I joined 'to set the people free'. I was one of the many
at that time recruited by this so-quickly forgotten slogan.
I had, after all, to make my choice between the two principal
protagonists, if I wished to make anything of my political
endeavours. In the one political corner was a Labour Government of mainly inexperienced politicians, hell bent on bringing
about the Socialist paradise within five years, meanwhile
continuing the absurd and unnecessary restrictions of food
rationing which nobody either respected or obeyed, thereby
corrupting the entire nation just as surely as the United States
had been corrupted by Prohibition twenty years previously—
and, likewise, enslaving my own profession by the legislation
of the National Health Service. In the other was the Conservative Opposition with the expansive personality of Lord
Woolton radiating *bonhomie* and liberal ideas—not to mention
a Churchill still in full possession of his faculties.

Who could doubt his choice?

The avuncular personal qualities of Woolton that had so
successfully built up the large department store business of
Lewis's dynamised the Conservative Party and its branches.
It became a band of hope, and a fraternity of love, united in
a single endeavour—to Set The People Free, to turn out the
Socialists.

'EVERYBODY WELCOME' was the sign which, in those
days, was hung over the door of the Conservative Central
Office.

Introduced as I was by David Eccles, it was a mere formality
for me to get my name on the list of parliamentary candidates.

The friendly Jim Thomas,** Party Vice-Chairman in charge
of the candidates' list, gave me a truly big hello on my entry.

* Subsequently Earl of Longford, Leader of the House of Lords.
** The late J. P. L. Thomas, Conservative M.P. for Hereford and later Lord
Cilcennin.

May be, even from his point of view, I was a prize—a proselyte from those troublesome Liberals, whose spoiling tactics of putting up their own candidates at Election time were bidding fair to thwart the otherwise 'inevitable' Conservative victory at the next General Election.

Unfortunately, however, it appeared that Jim Thomas had been giving a big hello to practically everyone who had come along during the previous couple of years, with the result that, as far ahead as two years before the General Election, all the vacancies in all the constituencies that were winnable, were filled. It was, it seemed, too bad that I had not come along a little sooner. There would have been no difficulty in placing me then. But, of course, there would be occasional vacancies turning up from time to time. The selection committees tended to go for the younger men, but still—and my mentor looked at me quizzically so that, though I was still only forty-five, I felt the shadow of the grave pass over me—you never knew your luck! How could he help me in the meantime?

I explained about my enthusiasm for political research and the creation of policy. I had, after all, just written and published *The End of Socialism* — a book whose first edition had sold out on publication.

'Go along to the Research Department,' came the reply. 'Go along and see X———'

Thus it was, only a few days later, that I found myself in the Conservative Political Centre Research Department in the old-fashioned building in Great Queen Street, and facing X——— as he sat at his desk in his small room overlooking St. James' Park. No motives of delicacy cause me to omit the name of the gentleman whom I saw there: it is merely that, over these many years, I have entirely forgotten it. He was, I have no doubt, a good introduction: possibly I was meeting one who is now a senior officer of the Department. He was then, however, young and austere-looking, and his welcome was a frosty one.

Undaunted, I explained my interest in political research. Though eliciting no great response, I continued, ill at ease, to talk about my publishing firm that I had by then started. Its main objects were political, I explained, but in the meantime, to make the thing go, I had to publish books on travel, cricket and 'all that rot'.

'You think that cricket is rot, then, do you?' queried the serious-looking young man in somewhat starchy fashion.

Oh, dear me! I tried to recover myself, but suddenly realising where I was, and that I was no longer with my former radical companions, I fumbled my reply.

There was a silence and I made my apologies and left.

I scarcely need add that my presence did not darken the doors of the Conservative Political Centre Research Department from that day to this. It was the first of my many failures to adjust.

Fortunately, my irreverent attitude to the national game, though it marked the grave of my prospects in the Research Department, was no bar to me on the Central Office list of candidates, inasmuch as I found myself short-listed and interviewed by an almost heady selection of constituency committees—North Ealing, West Fulham, Uxbridge, South Bedfordshire—all in quick succession. But, just as it was considered a good thing to select an ex-Liberal on the short list for interview by way of variety in the first place, so, in the light of the Liberal 'spoiling' tactics to which I have referred, it was an equally satisfying operation to turn an ex-Liberal down, once it came to the final choice. I can well remember the lady Chairman of the Uxbridge Association, following my interview with whose selection committee I arrived home (as Betty still reminds me) pale and shaken, honouring me by sending me a telegram to say that I was not wanted.

We—I say 'we' of set purpose, because the vogue for wife-inspection had already started with Conservative constituency associations and Betty had to accompany me on these particular excursions—eventually arrived in Nottingham during the course of the winter of 1949–50, short-listed for the vacancy in the South Nottingham constituency. We were met at the station by the agent and there was another potential candidate (so he explained) to be met also.

'This is Mr. William Rees-Davies,' said our guide in due

course as he manifested himself once more with his further charge.

The late-comer who had joined us in the waiting taxi was not lacking in self-assurance.

Billy Rees-Davies* held the floor in the taxi in just the same manner as I was to hear him hold the floor on so many subsequent occasions in the House of Commons.

'The last time—indeed, I think that it was the only time —I was in Nottingham was when I was bowled for a duck by Larwood on the County Ground,' he declared as he sank into his seat.

My heart sank. I was not to hear what Billy Rees-Davies said in his address to the assembled multitude of the South Nottingham Conservative Association. But, as I anticipated, he got the job.

There were two more journeys to Nottingham to see the Committees of the Rushcliffe Division. But the Rushcliffe Division chose Martin Redmayne** who, later to achieve parliamentary distinction in the capacity in which we shall meet him later in this book, was known in the Nottingham area at that time by reason of his sports emporium. Then, since the General Election of 1950 was rapidly approaching and we could not spend our time indefinitely travelling over the length and breadth of the country to no purpose, I withdrew my name from the list of parliamentary candidates.

*   *   *   *   *

It seemed for long enough as if the only possible use which the Conservative Party had for my services was that of a ward canvasser, as a rank-and-file member of the West-Central Ward branch of the Sutton and Cheam Association.

Ward canvassing was, indeed, good exercise. It was, moreover, an inexpensive evening's amusement, conveniently placed near home for Betty with her domestic cares. I often

* William Rees-Davies, later Conservative M.P. for Thanet Division of Kent.
** Subsequently Lord Redmayne following his defeat in Rushcliffe Division, General Election 1966. M.P. for Rushcliffe Division, 1950–66. Chief Government Whip, 1959–64.

thought wistfully that perhaps I might have found opportunity for rather wider scope with the Tories. However, at least, Betty and I could work together and there is, after all, nothing like starting at the bottom.

In due course, as I have told elsewhere, the opportunities opened out unexpectedly. One Ward Councillor became Independent. (It comes back to me now how easy it was, as one canvassed from door to door, merely to mention another name as the Party candidate.) Another Ward Councillor moved away from the district. If these two events had not happened, I could still have been walking round the West-Central Ward. But, in the event, I found myself by 1951 a Councillor of the Borough of Sutton and Cheam, and a member of the Central Executive Committee of the Sutton and Cheam Association.

This was upward progress. But how far and in what direction? Already, in those early 1950s, there was a Conservative Government in power and it was starting to set the people free: it did, indeed, go as far as abolishing food rationing and initiating Independent Television. But the salad days of Opposition were over and the single-minded purpose of the Central Executive Committee of the Sutton and Cheam Conservative Association was the somewhat limited one of supporting the Government (regardless of what the Government happened to be doing); and of raising money to keep the Association going, so that in turn it could raise money for itself. Any interruption of this beneficent process, such as trying to introduce political discussion into its meetings, was an unnecessary and time-wasting distraction. If one had any thoughts of a political nature, it was soon clear that it was as well to keep them to oneself. Ginger was not a fashionable commodity.

However, with an *ennui* which, alas, I could not always conceal from my colleagues, I stuck out the Council of the non-County Borough of Sutton and Cheam for some three to four years. Then, in 1954, thanks to the events which I have fully described in *A Doctor Returns*, there came the crisis in which either I had to retire from politics completely, or there was a more exciting alternative—I could take the chance of making an application to be reinstated on the Central Office list of parliamentary candidates and make a final bid to find a constituency and enter Parliament. I had arrived at that stage of exasperation when it didn't really matter which. It was one of those watersheds in one's affairs which occur every so often.

'Would you go as far as Carlisle?' said John Hare* looking at me rather doubtfully from the other side of his desk in the small Vice-Chairman's room in Conservative Central Office in Victoria Street.

I had previously stipulated that, on account of domestic ties, I would not take a constituency more than 100 miles away from London—and, of course, Carlisle is three times that distance. However, this time it was different. To escape from the constricted world of the Sutton and Cheam Council with its horizon bounded by model aeroplanes in the parks and holes in the footpaths, I would go almost anywhere.

'It's not an easy place to fill,' said John Hare with almost unique prescience. He seemed to shake his head over Carlisle. 'However, there's a large Liberal vote which you may be able to do something about.'

As the astute Party manager, it clearly appealed to him to put someone with my own Liberal credentials into Carlisle. The M.P. for Carlisle at that time was Alfred Hargreaves (Labour) with a majority of 3192 votes from the 1951 Election; but he held the seat on a minority vote, as at that Election there had been a Liberal vote of 5866.

In the outcome Betty and I found ourselves in the unaccustomed, but not unpleasant, position of being the only contenders to appear before the Carlisle Association for the vacancy as their candidate and, though certain doubts were expressed about the choice of 'wisdom rather than youth' (as one of our supporters so kindly put it), our adoption was *nem con* amidst an atmosphere of warm welcome and personal enthusiasm. Within three months of being in an apparently

---

* John Hare, Conservative M.P. for Sudbury Division of Suffolk, then Vice-Chairman of the Party. Subsequently Viscount Blakenham and Party Chairman.

hopeless political position and following years of frustrating experience the magic incantation had been uttered, the door of the treasure cave was swinging open and here we were standing at its mouth.

The Liberals had always been a problem in Carlisle. 'The Conservative had never won Carlisle with a Liberal candidate in the field', so it was quite erroneously said; and the Liberal candidate, Kenneth Wolstenholme, was a strong contender.

However, it seemed as if nothing could now stop the favourable trend of our fortunes. When the opportunity came to him of the appointment as Sports Commentator on the B.B.C., which he has now occupied for so many years, Kenneth Wolstenholme could scarcely be blamed for accepting this in the place of what was, at the best, a forlorn candidature. He was not replaced and, finally, just before the Election campaign of May 1955 started, it was announced that there would be no Liberal Party candidate on account of shortage of funds. It was a straight fight in Carlisle for the first time for many years.

As the record of the results of the 1955 General Election will confirm, I won Carlisle from the Labour Party by 370 votes. (Taken on a percentage basis in proportion to the votes cast, almost an identical margin to that by which I had lost the Chippenham by-election some twelve years previously.) Even the fact that the crowd standing out in the street below the Crown and Mitre balcony at 1.30 a.m. on Election night to await the result, had stayed there in expectation of a Labour victory rather than my own, and that the 'boos' prevailed over the 'cheers' on the announcement by the Returning Officer, failed to alter this. I had, after all, secured the Liberal vote—or, at least, the most substantial section of it. I had, for the time being, won the allegiance and support of all sections of the Carlisle Conservative Association. I was now basking, and for some time would continue to bask, in the admiration of all concerned as the victorious Member of Parliament. It seemed as if nothing could possibly go wrong—not as far as Carlisle was concerned, anyway.

Neither the officers of the Carlisle Conservative Association—nor any of its members—had so far even mentioned cricket in our conversations.

At last, I too could now help actively 'to set the people free'.

CHAPTER THREE

THE LOBBIES OF FRUSTRATION

T HUS, IN May 1965, practically twenty years to the day since I had first stood on a political platform as a parliamentary candidate at Bury, Lancashire, I found myself walking through the cloisters of Old Palace Yard and into the Members' Entrance, in response to the summons from the Chief Government Whip with its various underlines.

What now? Rather than repeat what I have written in *A Doctor in Parliament*, published during my first term in the House, let me call to witness Mr. Mark Bonham Carter giving his impressions of his own entry:

'It's just like being a new boy at public school—with its rules and rituals, and also its background of convention which breeds a sense of anxiety and inferiority in people who don't know the rules.' He makes the interesting remark that Labour M.P.s in particular are overawed by it. Indeed, it is true that, by 1955 anyway, the three periods of Labour Governments had not succeeded in making much permanent impact on an institution moulded essentially to the convenience of the traditional ruling class of British society.

For me, it was not only like school, but somehow the entrance cloisters and then the Members' stone balustraded staircase to the Principal Floor, with its three right-angle turns, were for all the world like my own school, Cheltenham College, of some forty years previously. By now I had spent years basking in the dignity and respect of professional life as a doctor, further years as the centre of admiration as a political candidate, and here I was at the age of fifty-two somehow or other back at Square One.

With unhappy reminiscences of these stultifying days of public school life at the beginning of the century as a prelude to my daily entry through the swing doors into the Members' Lobby, the tenseness of the atmosphere would hit me like a blow in the solar plexus. Throughout my first months in Parliament the resultant hollow feeling in the pit of my stomach could only be assuaged by continual glasses of cold milk at the tearoom counter, repeated at almost hourly intervals throughout the day. The cold milk eased my queasy feelings, but I cannot say that it brought me further benefit than that—it would perhaps have been better for my career, if not for my health, if I had penetrated a short distance further as far as the Smoking Room and started on whisky.

These were the days of the short-lived Government of Sir Anthony Eden, who had at last succeeded Sir Winston Churchill immediately prior to the General Election of May 1955. (Sir Anthony's photograph had been a real winner at the Election—we had distributed no less than 10,000 of a leaflet portraying this round the Council Estates of Carlisle.)

It was the Indian Summer of the Old Establishment. It may be 'old hat' to talk of the Old Etonians, but in 1955 the Old Etonians were the dominating factor. Not even Sir Winston's most fervent admirer can maintain that the radical fervour of his youth lasted through to his declining years and, at this point of time, 'the long march of the Common People' had reached the stage where nine out of the eighteen Cabinet Ministers in the Government of Sir Anthony Eden were Old Etonians: there being, in addition, yet more Etonians, as well as a plentiful sprinkling of hereditary peers, in other Government posts. The Prime Minister was an Old Etonian, the Leader of the House (The Right Hon. Harry Crookshank) was an Old Etonian, The Chief Whip (The Right Hon. P. G. T. Buchan-Hepburn) was an Old Harrovian. Even the Minister of Pensions, whose name I leave you to remember for yourself, was an Old Etonian. As important as all this, these members of a hereditary caste were supported by a solid cadre of eighty or more Old Etonians as members of the Conservative Parliamentary Party—not in all cases obtrusive people, but sufficient to permeate the atmosphere, to establish the ethos of the Party, to be ready with unwavering support for their schoolfellows in Government when needed.

With the great victory in 1945 at war, with the equally great political victory over the Socialists at the polls in 1951, the people had been 'set free'. But, as Christopher Hollis has pointed out, there was a greater proportion of Old Etonians in the Government of Sir Anthony Eden (and, of course, in the subsequent Governments of Mr. Harold Macmillan) than there were in the Governments thrown up by the unreformed Parliaments prior to 1832.

Perhaps here I should make the point in parenthesis that Parliament, so like a school with its curious disciplines and conventions, is not one school only, but two schools, each with its own methods and its own disciplines—its own secrecies and its own inhibitions. These schools are the two large Party machines and it is the interaction between them and between both of them together and the historic machine of Parliament, which makes the parliamentary scene as it is to-day. In the context of this book, the Party machines are the conspiracies that have swallowed Parliament to the extent that the battle of freedom has to be fought all over again. It is not only that, between them, they control parliamentary procedure and parliamentary disciplines (including a certain number of non-parliamentary disciplines of their own); but also that the Member's whole life is lived within the confines of his particular Party machine, which conditions him ruthlessly to its own purpose. The machines live side by side, but yet in isolation from each other. The average Member eats (the opposite ends of the long Members' Dining Room are respectively occupied as a routine by Conservatives and Socialists —there is the Conservative end and the Socialist end), drinks, talks, and spends the day—and sometimes far into the night— with his Party. This is the operative factor in the life of the Member. There are no rules, there is merely 'custom'— virtually unbreakable custom.

Where does Party end and where does Parliament begin?

Or *vice versa*? Has 'privilege', for instance, been used to shelter Party as well as Parliament?

How is it that so often—and so often, indeed, under Conservative Government—that those who are apparently the most able parliamentarians do not coincide with those who find high office in the councils of the nation? This was the never-ending puzzle to anyone concerned with the state of the nation during the 1930s—as it may well be even now to the student both of these years in retrospect and of the years about which I am now writing. It is, however, only by acceptance of the proposition that it is the secret processes of the Party that count first and last, while performance in the open parliamentary arena no longer has significance, that any understanding of the situation can be come by.

When I had fought the Chippenham Division of Wiltshire in the 1945 General Election as a Liberal Candidate, I used a slogan. This was embodied in a cartoon: in the foreground of the cartoon was a medium-sized figure of Winston Churchill, while towering over him in the back was a large, ugly looking animal on a lead. This animal was conspicuously labelled THE TORY PARTY and the caption underneath was 'LOVE ME, LOVE MY DOG'.

Then, as I have related, I joined the Tory Party myself— 'to set the people free'. In 1955 here I was in Parliament— I had to love the dog too. I did not find it, to start with, an easy thing to do.

Reginald Bevins, ex-Postmaster General and former Conservative Minister, in his *Sunday Express* articles of 1965 and in his subsequent book *The Greasy Pole*,* has averred that the power of the traditional British social and hereditary Establishment is founded on provisions contained in the Second Statute of Westminster of the year 1272. He may be right. But, irrespective of the events of the previous seven centuries, the Conservative Parliamentary Party of the 'fifties was undoubtedly the last stronghold of the class who at their zenith had ruled over a quarter of the land surface of the globe, but whose power was now draining rapidly away. These years saw them

* *The Greasy Pole*, by Reginald Bevins (Hodder and Stoughton, 1965).

in a tenaciously fought rearguard action against the forces
which were rising to engulf them. In the course of this, those
whom I have termed 'The Old Establishment' dominated
their contracted Empire in the lobbies of Westminster with
that same exclusive behaviour of an entrenched class they had
in a previous era exhibited in their broader Empire across the
seas. A Tory backbencher without family background, or
devoid of social pretensions, was the last of the colonials,
subjected to all the snubs and insults which, despite the
benevolence and humanity of British rule, have bequeathed
to us to-day our legacy of antagonism amongst former subject
peoples.

Let us in fairness not misunderstand the situation. It was
no solid totalitarian cadre that thus dominated the House of
Commons. For neither Eton nor the British aristocracy have
through the ages lacked variety of personality or of opinion:
the individualists and the eccentrics came in too. Indeed, one
sometimes wondered throughout the years whether, had it not
been that the eldest sons of earls were admitted to the House
of Commons (at that epoch they were still faced with in-
escapable translation to the House of Lords), there would
have been any real independence on the Conservative back-
benches at all.

It was rather that this cadre of people, both Government
establishment, independent thinker and eccentric, were united
by a way of life, and so formed a complete 'all-purpose'
parliamentary system—a culture of their own that dominated
and shaped Parliament so that the institution itself became
divergent in its ways and, as the twentieth century progressed,
remote from the world which surrounded it. The very light
above Big Ben seemed to shine out as a beacon of a past world
amongst the stormy seas of egalitarianism and scientific
advance which were eventually to engulf it. Thus, in the
cloistered atmosphere of this Victorian Gothic pile, with its
sombre lobbies, its overcrowding, its many 'conveniences' (for
months, so it seemed to a new Member, every fresh mysterious
door opened on to yet another gent's W.C.) and its even more
manifold inconveniences, it became possible for a ruling

community of grown men to go on living the life of a nineteenth-century boys' public school, that was so suited to its own particular purpose. Guarded by police and privilege, aloof from its surroundings, here was a monastic body as remote as if it had been on Mount Athos, but yet one which had to produce the rulers of a modern, twentieth-century industrial society.

'Etonians may dominate the Conservative Party but elsewhere they increasingly appear figures of fun', stated Malcolm Muggeridge scornfully in his review of Robert Wilkinson's book *The Prefects*. Yet, though they lost out eventually, the Etonians cannot be dismissed as lightly as that. Or, at least, one certainly could not dismiss them lightly in the Parliaments of the 1950s. One of the most successful conspiracies in the history of politics, they perished only through an extreme degree of maladjustment, bred of an extreme degree of arrogance, combined with an extreme degree of ill-luck. In the end, it was as if the Almighty Himself got fed up with the Old Etonians.

But, in 1955, in my position as a new entrant to the Conservative Party in Parliament, one could not avoid the feeling of being one of 'the lesser breeds without the law'. It can doubtless be proved statistically that not more than 50 to 100 Conservative M.P.s were, even then, actually related to each other, yet assembled with my new colleagues, whatever the occasion might be, I became imbued with the dismal feeling, which it took months, if not years, to overcome, that I was positively the only one excluded from a widespread cousinage.

Since my days at Cheltenham College I had lived my life in 'unestablished' backwaters—save for only a short period after the war when, thinking perhaps to pursue social ambitions, I had become a member of an exclusive golf club. It was gratifying indeed to obtain membership of such a club and look round the club house to see the photographs of former Prime Ministers and Lord Chancellors of England as *ci-devant* members. But it was only gradually that one got the hang of the thing, as one discovered that there was no social life attached to this club. One could pay one's subscription and, as a rightfully entitled member, play round the course: one had the facilities of the club house at one's disposal and could even use the lavatories. But the club had no social events: you could find no company in the bar at times when one might normally expect to find such company; you could not find anyone at any time who would be willing to discuss anything to do with the running of the club. (The Club Secretary was, of course, a 'sitting crow' and could not avoid an approach, but he would be careful to explain in the most polite terms that his Committee was a very difficult one in regard to anything you might suggest.) For all such things—indeed anything that mattered—were discussed only in select gatherings, the exclusive private cocktail parties which took place in the opulent-looking houses which surrounded the course. You could even enter the competitions and, if so be you were drawn to play against one of 'the magic circle', your opponent would be charm and friendliness itself throughout the round to such an extent that you would feel that you were really getting somewhere—until perhaps the following day you encountered the same person in the street and found that he cut you dead.

So with the upper echelons of the Conservative Party in those days. It would have been nice (one felt that they felt) to have kept the Parliamentary Party within the cousinage. But it could not be done in an era of universal suffrage. The course had to be kept up: it would go to pot without the extra subscriptions to pay for the upkeep. So the outsider had to be admitted. (My own entrance fee had been the extra Liberal votes in the marginal seat of Carlisle.) A price had to be paid for this: but as small a price as possible. The outsider could be allowed on to the course: and indeed into the club house. But for him to be allowed any social advantages from the Club, or any say in the running of it, that was another matter. Only the most careful scrutiny—a far closer scrutiny than that which seems to have been applied during these years to those who had access to national secrets—could provide the answer to this. Would the incomer be loyal to the Club? Not with just an ordinary loyalty, but with an unquestioning and abject attitude, in the course of which he must protest his loyalty as often and as publicly as possible? Would he be docile and uncomplaining in accepting in all circumstances the decisions of the Officers and the Committee? Even if these decisions were so absurd as to involve him in playing the course the right way round one day: and maybe in the reverse direction the following day? Was he single-mindedly devoted to the Club, without any allegiance to any other Club whatsoever? Would he conform, in his dress, in his conversation and in his general turn-out and appearance, to club standards?

As I have to explain, these were all points in which I failed miserably. In the intervals between consuming my glasses of milk in the tearoom, or musing over my comparisons with Cheltenham College of forty years previously and my exclusive golf club, I would ask myself: were these gloomy lobbies, with their schoolboy lockers on either side, indeed the corridors of power? (Or words to that effect, since this was 1955, pre-Snow, and this particular cliché was yet to find currency.)

Only reluctantly did I come to a negative conclusion. To have scaled the peak of achievement after so prolonged and arduous a climb, only to discover the ultimate goal still looming in the distance, separated as yet by inhospitable-looking valleys and formidable mountain ranges, was a bitter pill indeed.

Here, sitting on the back benches, one was only on the counterscarp, with the citadel still towering in front, guarded by its impregnable battlements and hordes of defenders. Indeed, the back benches below the gangway—which in nine years were as far as I ever ventured into the Debating Chamber —though forming a fine vantage point for observation, could be a cold and chilly place, as one watched over the years other and more fortunate colleagues find entry to the citadel— some, the favoured types, being welcomed at the main gate with ceremonial lowering of the drawbridge; others finding more devious paths through various postern gates, whether perhaps the one labelled 'Smoking Room', or that other

THE LOBBIES OF FRUSTRATION

involving its long crawl on hands and knees, labelled 'Private Parliamentary Secretaryship'.

Where then did the power lie? Was it here or was it there? As one gazed at the citadel wrapped in its mists of silence, only broken every now and then by the thud of a mangled political corpse as it came hurtling back over the battlements into outer space, one could, as a neophyte, not even guess. Was it with this proud Minister? Or with that disdainful back-bench figure? Both of whom, as Etonians—as, once again, *Westminster Confidential* put it so aptly—held the view that 'not only have Etonians the divine right to rule Britain, but also a virtual monopoly of the talent for doing so'.

There is no need whatsoever to personalise. Looking back, I have a curious memory of an impenetrable wall of faces, individually different maybe, but giving an identical collective impression—a stony stare, a defensive attitude with but one message. The message was: 'We are watching you. We are scrutinising you with each step that you take, with each drink that you drink, each word that you say. Do the right thing (but best of all, do nothing at all), say the right thing (but mind you don't say it out of turn!) and perhaps, maybe, one day, if we approve of you, we will let you in and give you a chance. We can't say how: we can't say when; but it will happen one day—that is, if you wait long enough.'

'But do the wrong thing, speak out of your turn, then, my boy, you're OUT, OUT for good!'

What was the right thing to do? What was the wrong thing to do? I did most of the wrong things, so perhaps I ought to know.

Harry Kerby, whose ready wit and impishly irreverent attitude were an ever-present antidote to all this, even from my earliest days in Parliament, had his own way of putting it. It was Harry's theory that, when you came into Parliament, you had an equal start, you had 'the lot' (as he put it) in reserve—an earldom, a viscountcy, a barony, a baronetcy, a knighthood, even the C.B.E. All these things would be added to you in due course, provided that you kept your record clean. But with every 'black' you made, each one was struck off in turn, until finally you were left an outcast—with nothing.

Naturally, in this equal race, it had to be admitted that some were more equal than others. But even I, at the start, was in the race.

Alas for my own chances in this inverted Grand National in which I was an entrant, I was to crash heavily at the first fence. It is anti-climax, sheer bathos in fact, to report that it was no Old Etonian, no true Romany, who was responsible for my discomfiture, but one, rather, of the recruits to the system in the shape of that emergent political wonder, Mr. Iain Macleod, appointed to the Government Front Bench and subsequently as Minister of Health, consequent on a single speech in Parliament.

Lest I have unwittingly given the impression of there being anything sinister or unpleasant in the vetting processes to which I have referred, let me say forthwith that no atmosphere could have been more pleasant or hospitable than that which prevailed at the round of tea-parties to which the new parliamentary entries at the 1955 Election were invited at various Establishment addresses. There was nowhere pleasanter indeed than the reception room of the late Lord Crookshank's charming house in Pont Street, S.W.1, where we, the new Conservative parliamentary recruits, had been invited to meet the Ministers. Unfortunately these were not the sort of occasions on which Betty (for wives had been invited also) and I greatly shone: and on this particular occasion it was not easy to overcome the sense of strain and the feeling that we were, once again, new boys at school being invited to an initiation tea-party in the Headmaster's drawing-room.

We were therefore occupying our customary reticent place on the edge of the crowd, talking merely to each other. But here, giving us a 'big hello' of welcome was a squat and squarish figure, streaking across the room beaming to make my acquaintance. I had recognised Iain Macleod and who knows what benevolent intention may have at that moment filled the mind of Mr. Iain Macleod?

But, after he had introduced himself as 'Macleod, Minister

of Health', I opened with what I fondly imagined to be a normal conversational gambit:

'I am hoping to have a few Questions to ask you . . .' I started.

As I write this, I read Iain Macleod's statement at the Young Conservatives' Conference at Brighton on 16th January 1965. 'It is more important to argue than to agree', declared Mr. Macleod.

However, Iain Macleod could not have been thinking up this future speech at that particular moment, for, at the mention of the word 'Question', the beam disappeared from his face as if an electric light bulb had been switched off and he strode quickly away without a single word. Though he was Minister of Health for a further twelve months, and we encountered each other frequently in the lobbies, I was not to exchange another word with Iain Macleod for a matter of some eight years—except for the numerous Questions which I asked him at Question Time.

It was perhaps tactless of me to have acted as I did. But I had already decided, in spite of the formidable discouragements which I have enumerated, to go my own way and to make use of the facilities which I had been granted as a Member of Parliament. I had, in fact, many Parliamentary Questions for the Minister of Health—I was to ask some hundred or more on the subject of mental health alone. It was a matter of assessing my position from a common sense point of view. At the age of fifty-two I was a hopelessly late entry. I had been elected as a Government Member by only 370 votes— votes which, in accordance with all the customary odds on the swing of the electoral pendulum, would melt like snow at the next General Election. Perhaps, with ten years off my age and another few thousand on my majority, it would have been worth my while to make the long, cool bid for the rewards of good and docile behaviour. But with the prospect of only a single, short term in Parliament and a problem of desperate urgency—that of the laws relating to mental health— on my hands, I must defy the lightning and go ahead.

I have written an account of my campaigning on this question in *A Doctor in Parliament*.

In conclusion of this chapter I need only mention that, following this first round of parties, I received no further invitations to any selective Establishment parties throughout my entire time in Parliament: nor, come to that, was my name ever included during the whole of my nine years in any of those parliamentary delegations abroad which, for the average M.P., combine prestige with enjoyment in so delectable a fashion. Though I can scarcely go so far as to blame Mr. Iain Macleod for this.

CHAPTER FOUR

THE REGRESSION OF THE CONSERVATIVE PARTY

IN THE face of such insurmountable obstacles as I have described where could the aspiring politician have found guidance? What had the oracle to say as to the attainments required to enter the citadel? This is on record—if not at the precise moment of time which I have reached in my story, then at any rate only a year or so later.

Mr. Quintin Hogg, then Lord Hailsham and Chairman of the Conservative Party, defended the selection of Conservative candidates in an article in the *Sunday Times* of 23rd January 1959. While leaning over backwards to emphasise that 'we ought to have in the House of Commons the widest possible range of experience, representative of the nation and the different kinds of social, family, educational and economic backgrounds', he stated that 'the best age for launching out on a parliamentary career would in his estimate be somewhere between thirty and forty'.

'We need', wrote Lord Hailsham, 'people who understand industry and commerce, but we do not want the Party to be exclusively formed of them: and they should reach Parliament before they are too rigid and set in their ways, otherwise they find difficulty in adapting themselves to political life.

'I have read', admitted the writer, 'some critical comments which suggest that Conservative M.P.s and candidates are drawn from too narrow a social background. I do not believe that most of this criticism is justified.'

I do not suppose that Lord Hailsham was thinking specifically of me in his remark in the second paragraph of this quotation, but he might have been.

What makes the Tory Party tick?

Any Socialist will give the answer. It is in his view quite simply 'the vested interests', meaning the financial and industrial vested interests—the interests of those who exploit the workers for their own gain. Perhaps at one time he would have been right. He would have been right, for instance, in reference to the Tory Parliamentary Party between the wars and the businessmen who supported Baldwin and Chamberlain —themselves both businessmen. But he has been only partly right in the post-war world. As Lord Hailsham has made amply clear in his statement, another interest stepped in after the war, that of the Party managers (drawn, of course, from the best people) telling the financiers and the industrialists where they get off, so to speak. Telling them, in effect: 'We will still allow you to subscribe your cash, but you must leave this business of government to us. We and our forebears have been doing this thing for some three to four hundred years—even longer. We will mind the shop: we will look after you—that is, when we can. But we do not want a lot of unadaptable people who interfere with our ways.' And the financiers and industrialists tamely agreed. They subscribed to this bargain, less worse befall. Though, in the outcome, they have been treated rather shabbily. Even under a Conservative government they had some nasty knocks, both as to their vested interests and in regard to their direct representatives finding places in Parliament and in government.

Thus, the businessmen, who were so easy a target in the Parliaments of the 'thirties were swept aside in favour of a worthier if somewhat more archaic concept—rule by the best people, the hereditary and social aristocracy, and those who by arduous endeavour have assimilated themselves to it. The Etonians, in fact. So, while other nations moved into the twentieth century, Britain turned back the political clock to the days before the industrial revolution.

Who are the representatives of the best people? Ideas on this clearly varied as between the free and easy days in Opposition when I first entered Conservative Central Office in the 1940s and the time when the Party was in Government in the subsequent decade. To ascertain them, we must identify the survivors, first of Central Office scrutiny (the modern tenets of which are so clearly set out by Lord Hailsham); second, of the fine sieve of the constituency selection committees in their choice of prospective candidates; finally, of the still finer selection of their potential successors by those in authority at the very top—the ultimate choosing of those whose feet are to be placed firmly on the escalators of public life, so that, what'er befall, they are from then on bound to move upwards. For, let there be no misapprehension, none of these things happens by accident in the Tory Party.

In the post-war years each 'philosopher-king' of the Party endeavoured in turn to fashion the Party image in accordance with his own ideas and his own personality, with the objective of replacing the tarnished memory of the pre-war Conservative Party and its middle-aged businessmen.

'So, having trained a succession of others like themselves whom they can leave to be the guardians of the State, they can depart to the isles of the blessed and live there.'

The *Daily Telegraph* editorial movingly quotes Plato on the occasion of Lord Butler's retirement from politics. But the same quote can apply to Mr. Harold Macmillan or even to Lord Woolton: and, indeed, does apply in both cases.

Let us start with Lord Woolton—for it was he, with his genuine democratic sense and his economic philosophy of the Manchester School, who opened the gates of Central Office to the newer generation of independent business and professional men, regardless of their social origins, who, imbued with the conception of 'setting the people free', flooded into Parliament on the tide of victory in the General Elections of 1950 and 1951 —even in that of 1955.

The academically minded Rab Butler, simultaneously in charge of the Conservative Research Department, saw the Party leadership, on the contrary, in the shape of a progressively minded middle-class intellectual *élite*. No longer were the leaders of Conservatism to be overlaid with social pretensions, or to be tainted by the fleshpots—'the pore scholar', after the best medieval fashion, was to be the new ideal towards Conservative regeneration. Undoubtedly, Rab Butler's establishment of the Conservative Research Department and its personnel in the days of Opposition between 1945 and 1951 had a vital effect on the rehabilitation of the Party.

However, important as the protagonists of the 'One World Movement'—who now form the Party leadership—were to become in due course, neither the Woolton, nor the Butler dispensations were of anything more than marginal importance when the Conservative Party regained power in 1951 for, already safely ensconced in the places of power, were the occupants of the 188 safe Conservative parliamentary seats, mainly country seats, who had survived the 1945 Election. It is the basic fact about the Conservative Party, to be ignored at one's peril, that these seats are firmly held by the entrenched classes. 'The knights of the shires' were no mere phantasy of political correspondents: they were the hard core of the Party, the holders of the Conservative strongholds. It was from this *élite* that the new Conservative Government of 1951 was drawn: and it became the assumption that Great Britain was to be governed in the modern age under the rule of an oligarchy comparable only to that of medieval Venice.

There was, moreover, no way within the Party machinery by which this assumption could be gainsaid.

Throughout the decades, it had been the tradition of the Conservative Party that, once the Party was in Government, intellectual activity, which could only lead to questioning and disunity, to disharmony and conflict with the Party leadership, should cease and be replaced by an unquestioning and un-critical loyalty to the Party Leader, who had now become Prime Minister, and to his chosen Ministers. This can well be ascribed to the not entirely unpraiseworthy reaction of a body of high-minded people. Though whether it was to the ultimate interest of a Party whose intention was to remain in power over a long period of time is a more questionable proposition. For, as this book will show, it was to set up stresses and strains of an intolerable character within the Conservative Party of the late 1950s and early 1960s. It was, moreover, to ensure the alienation of the entire class of political intellectuals whose support the Party could ill afford to lose.

Its immediate effect, however, was one that could only be gratifying to those who had inherited the oriflamme of power. For, when an association of men and women ceases to cerebrate as the Conservative Party organisation was called upon to do in its new function as a totalitarian political machine, the bond between them can no longer be one of ideas or of principles—particularly when such principles are compromised by the exigencies of Government—and other factors enter to fill this ideological vacuum. It was not long, in fact, before the enthusiasm for freedom, so assiduously fanned in Opposition, but so quickly slaked in Government, was replaced by an obsessional regard for archaic forms of social distinction and the trivia of political patronage. In the absence of any concept beyond that of an unquestioning regimental loyalty, these became the cement that held the Party together.

It is our pride that 'the spoils system' does not exist in British politics. Thus, for the leaders of any victorious Party, it must always have been a comforting thought, once the few jobs at his disposal are handed out, how easy it can be to satisfy the remainder of his followers with a handful of knighthoods, and a further sprinkling of C.B.E.s, O.B.E.s and M.B.E.s, which cost nothing at all. It is an additional asset when, as has been the case with the Conservative Party, the loyal troops of the political army are so enamoured of social distinction that they are prepared to slave themselves to the bone as political workers for the opportunity of an invitation to a tea party at which the Duchess of Z—— is present, or for the sake of a handshake with Lady Y——.

Maybe as over-compensation for the rapid disappearance of financial differentials between themselves and their social inferiors which was the feature of these years, the politically active section of the British middle class did not take unkindly to this system.

It was the great day in the life of our friend, Miss A——, when she and a relative journeyed up to London to visit the Palace to receive the well-merited decoration for 'political and public services'. Betty and I had hoped that it would enhance the occasion for them to lunch at the House of Commons to celebrate an event in which, by my previous recommendations, I had played a little part. So it turned out, but Betty and I, as hosts, were left with the feeling that the visit to Westminster was marked, not so much by our own company in the Strangers' Dining Room, but rather for the vision which had been granted to them simultaneously with our meeting them in the Central Lobby. The vision was that of a handsome young man with reddish hair, with the slim head and figure of a well-bred greyhound—it was that of the Earl of Dalkeith, Conservative Member of Parliament for Edinburgh, North—and at that time, reputedly one of the escorts of Princess Margaret. The lunch with us was just a happy and friendly occasion: the sight of the Earl of Dalkeith was bliss incomparable.

There is another occasion that stays in mind: that of the selection of the new candidate in the safe seat from which the elderly Member, full of years and honours, was retiring. (Surprisingly enough, this was a Parliamentary constituency in one of London's new suburbs, in a totally non-traditional area.) The Selection Committee, guided by the Chairman and the Agent, had made their choice after laborious investigation: and there were three candidates. There was the successful businessman-politician of humble origin, who deserved well of the Party in as much as he had fought and all but won on two occasions 'a Labour marginal': there was the talented son of the distinguished Minister of State: then there was the equally talented, but entirely inexperienced, younger man with the striped blue on black (Etonian) tie, the West End address and the social background. The Chairman reviewed the qualifications of each in turn in front of the fifty-strong Association Executive. It was an even contest of merit: but there was one decisive factor. When the Chairman and Agent, out of bounden duty to the Association, had allowed themselves to be entertained in the home surroundings of each candidate in turn, at the West End address of the third candidate they too had seen a vision—this was his wedding photograph on the piano in which, amongst the principal guests, there had been included the Queen Mother. It was candidate Number Three who got the vote.

'Moreover', said the Chairman as he announced and congratulated the candidate. 'I shall not be surprised if we see our future Member chosen for office within a comparatively short time of his election to the House."

The Chairman was quite right. He was.

But I ought not, I suppose, to complain. Even for me opportunity knocked in this strange new world, had I but accepted it.

It was while I was still a candidate in 1954 that I received a list of the names of Conservative parliamentary candidates being circulated by Conservative Central Office in connection with some extremely worthy function. My consternation can well be imagined when I looked it through and was unable to find my name. Had I been disinherited and struck off the roll? I started to ask myself as I scanned the letter 'J's. I could think of no other explanation until suddenly, out of the corner of my eye, I caught sight of a familiar-looking name under letter 'M'. Could this be me? Yes, it *was* me in strange guise, as if here I was, wearing padded shoulders to my coat, pointed shoes and quiffed hair; inasmuch as, by strange Central Office alchemy, my name had been changed from my customary signature to 'D. McIntosh (hyphen) Johnson', so that I numbered amongst the 'M's. It was the occasion of considerable distress to the appropriate department of Central Office, where they had undoubtedly been doing their best for me, when I phoned to say that I did like to regard myself as plain 'Johnson', without any hyphens, and would they be so kind, etc. etc.? Alas for my initial 'difficulty of adaptation'! Who knows how different this story might have been, had I allowed myself to be moulded into shape as 'McIntosh-Johnson'?

*   *   *   *   *

Thus it was that, with the Old Etonians in the seats of power, with the Conservative Associations devoted to the political line dictated by the Leader of the Party and his Ministers, whatsoever that line might be, and conditioned as if they were

Pavlov's dogs to a positive reaction of acclamation at the sight of the black tie with its blue stripe, the aristocratic control of the Conservative Party seemed assured. Patronage, the pursuit of social prestige, unquestioning loyalty to the Prime Minister for the time being, whoever he might be, and whatever policy he pursued, were the things that made the Party in the country 'tick', irrelevant of what appeared in the Party literature, which, impressive as was both its quantity and the quality of its content, was largely left unread—hanging about forlornly on the tables of Conservative Committee Rooms, its only serious students being political opponents who came to regard it as an almost indispensable source of information. (I can well recollect debating against Mr. George Brown in Carlisle on the Health Service as a result of my accepting a comprehensive challenge thrown out in the House of Commons in the latter's characteristic expansive fashion: his 'Bible' on that occasion was the current C.P.C. pamphlet on the National Health Service!)

In the first Parliament with a Conservative majority there was little sign as yet of the schism which was to become the distressing feature of the subsequent two Parliaments—the schism between a compromising Government, conducting its affairs by political expediency, and the 1950 cadre of 'Woolton' backbenchers. All were for Freedom! To start with, anyway. Rationing was abolished, the Ministry of Food was wound up, controls and regulations were discarded in hundreds. Independent TV was established. Finally, in 1954, there was Crichel Down (that now all-but-forgotten place!). At the time it occurred, Crichel Down was looked upon as the bright dawn, another Runnymede. It was the victory of the individual, Lieut-Commander George Marten, over an arrogant and unscrupulous bureaucracy: the victory of Parliament, a single parliamentarian, the late Robert Crouch, Member for North Dorset (an historically individualist county) over a somewhat lackadaisical Minister of Agriculture, Sir Thomas Dugdale,* who resigned as a consequence of this incident.

Bob Crouch, gruff voiced and direct in his approach, an

* Subsequently Lord Craythorne.

independently minded person native to the historically independent-minded part of the country which he represented, was my first friend in Parliament. He and I somehow gravitated to the same part of the Chamber to take our seats—the corner seats adjacent to the gangway furthest from the Speaker's Chair, where one could slip in and out without being noticed, yet see what was going on and be ready to intervene as occasion arose.

Betty and I stayed the week-end with Bob and Kathleen at their farm a few miles north of Blandford and we duly made our pilgrimage to see Crichel Down. But the picture which I took of Bob Crouch with this temporarily well-known place as background scenery is one of the more forlorn exhibits in my photograph album. For there were to be no more Crichel Downs and Crichel Down, far from being a landmark in political history, is but a dusty memory even these dozen years later. While Bob himself died in a diabetic coma within a year of that date. Prior to his death he had lent me his Crichel Down papers for research and they lie mouldering in my attic, not worth the undoing even for the purpose of this book. Nor, even at the mention of this fact here, do I anticipate any rush of demand from the archivists.

Those who waited expectantly for greater victories for liberty following Crichel Down, were to wait in vain. For the Old Etonians, admirable as might have been their predecessors' demeanour on the field of Waterloo in the early nineteenth century, were manifestly failing to produce the officer material in the parliamentary battlefield of the mid-twentieth. Dogged and determined spirits and knowledgeable minds were needed to press forward against the Socialist foe in the twin battle for restoring liberty at home and staying the dissolution of the British Empire overseas. But, in contrast to this, Minister after Minister appeared deficient in both the brain-power and the experience to cope with his job in any other sense than being the spokesman of his Department: while, disdainful as he might be of his own subordinate backbenchers, he conspicuously lacked the heart for the contest against the enemy on the opposite side of the House of Commons. (Those deplorable

winding-up speeches against a yelling and deriding Socialist
Opposition—the most desperate memories of my nine years in
the House!)

Surrender to socialism and clamant trade unionism at home,
and to United Nations internationalism abroad, became the
order of the day. While this sorry state of affairs was camouflaged by such specious pretexts as that 'we must accept the
Welfare State' or that 'the task of a Conservative Government
is to show ourselves the better administrators of the Welfare
State than the Socialists'.

Thus (under the aegis of Mr. Iain Macleod, first Conservative Minister of Health after the 1951 Election) the
Socialist health service of Aneurin Bevan was swallowed whole,
totally undigested into any recognisable brand of Conservative
philosophy, discarding in the process such encumbrances as
the Conservative pre-election promises of drugs for private
patients; trade unions' demands for higher wages were granted
in wholesale fashion without serious attempt to ensure increased productivity or to restrain irresponsible unofficial
strike action; nationalised industries were unfettered either in
spending or in trading in competition with private enterprise;
while welfare statism and bureaucracy remained rampant and
uncontrolled throughout other spheres of national life.

*   *   *   *   *

When the dead hand of authoritarianism crushed original
thought throughout the Conservative Party and it became
social cachet, rather than intellectual attainment, that was the
necessary quality for advancement, what wonder that a gulf
appeared between Conservatism and all forms of intellectual
thought and speculation? The wholesale recruitment of the
influential intellectual classes to socialism can be well understood.

Likewise, when discussion amongst the ranks of the Party
was discouraged, when Ministers themselves had little time
to ponder on account of their day-to-day duties, when individual thought was proscribed as dissidence—and disloyalty

to the Party to boot—there was a vacuum left which others hastened to fill. These were the policy-making bureaucrats of the Government Departments, influenced in turn by their assiduous Socialist intellectual advisers. In the late 1950s this is what started to happen. In one sphere of national life after the other, any realistic Conservative M.P. found himself witness of the paradoxical spectacle of departmental policy— usually of a socialistic nature—being adopted by acquiescent Ministers and subsequently dished up in garish form in Conservative Political Centre pamphlets as Conservative Governmental policy, to be adopted without question by the Party faithful.

I would be hesitating to ventilate such outrageous ideas, were they not supported by more authoritative voices than my own. For in due course the doom of Conservative Government was presaged by the commentaries of those who, previously muzzled by the enforced silence of office, now, rid of this burden, felt themselves free to comment: the Earl of Kilmuir sums up the malaise of the administration in his book *Political Adventure** published in 1964:

'After ten years of power,' wrote Lord Kilmuir, in suitably euphemistic language, 'there was a too dominant preoccupation with administrative matters. Ministers had become obsessed with the work of their own departments and the Government as a whole lost interest in political thinking and the impact of the measures they proposed on ordinary people.'

What was the outcome? I find my report made for me by the political correspondent of *The Financial Times* in the issue of that paper of Monday, 6th April 1964, in reference to a commentary on the contemporary situation by Mr. Enoch Powell:

'Yet Mr. Powell is reflecting a widespread unease in the Party that Conservatives have for the moment lost their essential identity . . .

'It is not so much that the rank and file actively disagree with many of the Government policies, which seem to be more

---

* *Political Adventure: The Memoirs of the Earl of Kilmuir* (Weidenfeld and Nicolson, 1964), pp. 320, 321.

characteristically "leftish" than Tory. It is rather that they have failed to arouse the right response in the Conservative Party which, one suspects, is left with a sense that many of them have been forced on it.

'When the Conservatives came back to power after the fall of the 1945 Labour Government, every one in the Party had an instinctive grasp of what it stood for—economic progress and expansion in freedom, decontrol and a new chance for the individual after a period of collectivism. These aims united all shades of the Party.

'But now the Conservatives seem to feel themselves to be producing too many echoes of other people's policies.'

* * * * *

However, all this is but the stage-setting for the principal actor in our drama, who has been waiting in the wings, but who must now claim the centre of the stage.

CHAPTER FIVE

THE ERA OF MR. HAROLD MACMILLAN

IT WAS in January 1957, against the backcloth of the Suez crisis, whose parliamentary manifestations I have described in *A Doctor in Parliament*, there dropped on to the scene, as if a *deus ex machina*, the extraordinary figure of Mr. Harold Macmillan—'Super-Mac', who, as the cartoonists had it, could fly through the air with the greatest of ease.

Nobody had expected Harold Macmillan to become Prime Minister: indeed, nobody had expected Sir Anthony Eden to resign until almost the day of this sad *dénouement*. The Conservative succession on this occasion was settled swiftly, and decisively—there was no shenaniging in the tragic post-Suez days of December 1956 and January 1957. And to be fair, the result would have been the same, even if the up-to-date procedure of choosing the Tory leader had been in force. Rab Butler had been the acknowledged 'second man' to Eden, to the extent that during the Suez crisis he had answered for the Prime Minister in the House of Commons at many crucial moments during which the sick leader had been unable to appear. It was he who had had the invidious task of announcing the final withdrawal of British troops and the handover to the United Nations: and the association of ideas in this connection was of no help to him.

In any case, Rab Butler, a withdrawn figure, seldom seen in the House of Commons Smoking Room, or in the more exclusive West End clubs, the idol of the Progressives, was suspected, rightly or wrongly (and, for all I know, it could have been wrongly), of over-much sympathy with those forces of national defeatism which had inflicted so bitter a humiliation.

The event was all too recent and the right wing of the Parliamentary Party, in those days some 80 per cent or more of the Party, regardless of any consideration of social levels, would not have Butler. Harold Macmillan, paradoxically enough as it may now seem, swept in on a wave of right-wing indignation, which had been assessed, and correctly assessed, by Edward Heath as Chief Government Whip. Though nobody went out of their way to ask me my views on the leadership, I must none the less dispel the most common, but at the same time most erroneous, interpretation of these events which has it that the accession of Mr. Macmillan was brought about through a plot concocted by the Marquess of Salisbury and a small clique of unknown aristocrats. On an issue such as that of Suez, the non-U members of the Party were even more right-wingish than the aristos and, expressing themselves, as they did, to the Chief Whip, it was they primarily who ensured that Macmillan became Prime Minister—only later to discover that, with this chameleon-like politician, they had muffed their choice.

I had no ballot paper in any election for leadership in January 1957, but I would, in fact, have voted for Harold Macmillan if I had had one. It has not often been my lot to meet socially the members of the higher echelons of the Conservative Party, but I had met Harold Macmillan at a memorable juncture. This was at a private dinner party at the Conservative Conference at Blackpool in 1946 at that point in my career when, having left the Liberal Party, I was still to decide my next step. When this latter fact came up in conversation, I found myself the exclusive target of one of those splendid dissertations of which at a later date the nation as a whole, rather than a single individual of little consequence, became the recipient. The chosen text on this occasion: individual enterprise and its importance as a way of life, with special reference to the Macmillan Scottish crofter grandparent and his founding of the famous publishing firm. It was so sonorous, so convincing, that it had an important influence on my final decision the following year to espouse the Conservative cause.

Therefore, had anybody bothered to ask me, I too would

have supported Harold Macmillan for the Prime Ministership. Indeed, both I and my friends entertained the hope that, innovator that he had proved himself to be, he would shake up the stagnant set-up in which we were spending our frustrated existence. So, of course, he did. But not in the way that we had so hopefully anticipated.

It is by no means impossible that, had private enterprise and individual liberty been the political ethos of the day, Mr. Harold Macmillan would have weighed in with a policy based on these. But he was to show himself a man with shrewd appreciation of power and where power lay. He must at an early date in his Prime Ministership have formed a healthy respect for those extra-parliamentary forces which had overwhelmed the unfortunate Sir Anthony Eden—not to mention the intra-parliamentary force of those younger recruits to the Conservative Parliamentary Party, in regard to whom it sometimes seemed that any vacuum in their syllabus at Eton had been filled in by readings from the Yellow Books of Mr. Victor Gollancz—as far as Colonial and Foreign Affairs were concerned, anyway.

'Though a man of traditional values', stated *The Financial Times*' encomium on Mr. Macmillan's retirement seven and a half years later, 'Mr. Macmillan was totally modern and pragmatic in his approach and found no difficulty in presiding over a Government which saw the conversion of the Tory Party to planning.'

It was soon clear, even to a credulous person such as myself, that there was a yet more dominant strain in the Macmillan character than that of the grandson of the humbly born entrepreneur.

When Mr. Richard Marsh, Labour M.P. for Greenwich, in the debate in the House of Commons on 18th June 1964, read the following extract: 'The Socialist remedy should be accepted in regard to industries and services where it is obvious that private enterprise has exhausted its social usefulness or where the general welfare of the economy requires that certain basic industries and services need now to be conducted in the light of broader social considerations than the profit-making motive,' honorable Members on the Conservative benches are on record as shouting 'Karl Marx'.

But, no, the writer of these words was not the bearded revolutionary, but the well-connected young man of progressive tendencies, who in his day was so seriously misunderstood by his contemporaries and elders—it was Harold Macmillan, the Old Etonian with ducal relatives-in-law, writing in *The Middle Way*—yet another of those political testaments of the inter-war years of which insufficient notice was taken.

What more natural than that, now he had come to power in his maturity, the Macmillan Government, the Macmillan Party and the Macmillan Parliament should be fashioned after the image of the young Macmillan himself?

Youth—Progressiveness (not entirely to be confused with Progress)—The Middle Way—The Wind of Change: these were now to be the symbols for the rule of the best people. The Welfare State could only be entrusted to the well-born: the Wind of Change must essentially have those of superior social status as its vehicle. 'To mix with Kings, yet keep the common touch. To hob-nob with Dukes, yet set the key to Progress and Enlightenment.' This was to be the magic Macmillan formula, so successful over the years. For, progressive and enlightened as he might be, Mr. Macmillan still kept his Cabinet packed with Old Etonians.

Let us see, step by step, how the nostrum worked.

     ★   ★   ★   ★   ★

It is not easy to determine the exact point when the winds of change started to blow with hurricane force through the mental processes of Mr. Harold Macmillan.

First, there was the reconnaissance—a reconnaissance in depth, which went hand-in-hand with the rehabilitation of the Conservative Party. There was no more assiduous luncher-out —even if only as far as the Socialist end of the Members' Dining Room—than Tony Barber* a junior Whip, but now

* Anthony Barber, then Conservative M.P. for Doncaster. Subsequently Economic Secretary to the Treasury, later Minister of Health. Defeated, General Election, 1964. M.P. for Altrincham Division of Cheshire, 1965.

the Prime Minister's Parliamentary Private Secretary. Bland, charming and shrewd, conscientious and helpful, Tony Barber included in his survey even those whom, in his disarming fashion, he designated to their faces as 'the lunatic fringe'. Such skilled psychotherapy as this undoubtedly played an important part in the process of 'nursing the Party back to health'.

There was the feeling that, with this lively experimenter who now controlled our destinies from 10 Downing Street, something new would happen and nobody knew quite in which direction the cat was going to jump. Meanwhile all had high hopes.

In March 1957 the Marquess of Salisbury resigned from the Government over the question of the release of Archbishop Makarios. But the resignation of Lord Salisbury, in retrospect a milestone in British politics, passed virtually without comment, even in Conservative Party circles. While it was a sign of changing times that, as far as the British electorate were concerned, Lord Salisbury was virtually sunk without trace.

In 1958 Peter Thorneycroft and Enoch Powell went also. This was 'a little local difficulty' and that was all.

By this time the direction of the wind could be ascertained. Thus far, Conservative Government had relied upon a passive retreat before Opposition—giving way to trade union pressures for higher wages, giving way to the sponsors of collectivist and welfare policies at home, giving way to pressures on Suez and Africa abroad—the familiar expediencies of Ethelred and Unready and the Danegeld. But clearly there was a trick in the game that was worth two of that. Namely that a Conservative Prime Minister, rather than appear to be continually retreating, should, while still leading his own troops, turn his horse completely and place himself in the van of 'progress'.

Why resist the prevailing winds of politics—only to be in the end overcome by *force majeur*, as Eden had been—when one could place oneself at their head and ride before the gale?

Why, indeed, allow the policies of progress and the Middle Way to be in the hands of the *sans culottes*, the indifferently educated hordes of the Labour Party, when here were the

younger scions of the intelligent, the selectively educated and
well-bred, all eager to adopt them?

Why permit the outworn prejudices of an older generation
to stand in the path, when they could be so easily sterilised
by the call of Party 'loyalty' and Party discipline? The appeal
to Party loyalty assumed, and assumed correctly, that it was
loyalty *to the Leader* rather than to the principles of the Party
that would prevail. (There was, in the outcome, at no time
any conspicuous sign of conflict on this point in the Conservative Associations throughout the country.)

The Conservative Party after 'Suez' was demoralised,
overhung by the sour smell of defeat and disappointment.
The Party image was tarnished as it had scarcely been
tarnished during the century, even at the time of Munich.
But now the formula of progressive well-bred youth leading
the way—the Middle Way—to the New Jerusalem was to
provide the detergent that would wash the Party image
'whiter than perfect whiteness'. It was to be the electoral
nostrum that would induce that formidable, if somewhat
elusive, political figure, 'the middle of the road man', to vote
Conservative at Election time. Indeed, it may have succeeded
in doing this at the 1959 Election: though at an ultimate cost
that is still incalculable.

*   *   *   *   *

Where did the power lie throughout the years following
'Suez'?

There can be only one answer to this question. The power
lay with Mr. Harold Macmillan. Whichever way one looked,
whatever path one explored to find the explanation of this
happening or that happening, there at the end of the road
(even if one did not reach the road's end until long after the
event and after taking devious ways and being lost in almost
impenetrable jungles of hypocrisy and camouflage) was,
undoubtedly, Mr. Harold Macmillan. With power exercised,
if not directly, then at second, third or even fourth remove.

It was still the days of my own political innocence and a fine day in late May of 1959. This particular fine day of the Whitsun recess found me on the quay at Esbjerg on my way home from my pilgrimage to Copenhagen to see the Danish Ombudsman, Professor Hurwitz, prior to my asking the Prime Minister (Mr. Harold Macmillan, of course) a few days later on 11th June my Question in Parliament about the appointment of an Ombudsman in Britain*—a question which sowed the random seed which was to blossom in such promising fashion in subsequent years, though alas, in other hands than those of either Mr. Macmillan and myself.

I was wending my way across from the boat train to the m.v. *Kronprincesse Ingrid* which lay at the quayside ready to take us to Harwich on the last stage of this pleasant journey, when a big hello from a by-no-means unfamiliar voice fell upon my ear. I looked round to see that equally familiar car with its famous registration NAB (1, 2 or 3—I forget which) and, inside it, my colleague, friend and mentor, Gerald Nabarro.†

This was well met. In the course of the pressure of day-by-day business in the House of Commons, the opportunities were few when one could button-hole so preoccupied a colleague as Gerald Nabarro for a talk. Now, however, happily settled on the deck of m.v. *Kronprincesse Ingrid*, as we sailed out into the open sea, there was all the time in the world (or at least all the time until the following afternoon) for political chat. How natural that we should review the prospects for the forthcoming General Election which was, of course, to take place a few months later in October.

It would be wrong for it to be thought that the cause of traditional Conservatism and private enterprise was a 'dead duck' immediately after the Suez crisis. Indeed, a feature of the 1955–59 Parliament on the Government side of the House had been the welling up of revolt amongst that section of

---

* At the Ombudsman Celebration Dinner, on 30th November 1966, Tom Sargent, Secretary of 'Justice', was kind enough to attribute to the above question the impetus of Government interest that set on its feet his own work and that of his Society which led to Sir John Whyatt's Report and the eventual designation of Sir Edmund Compton as first British Ombudsman in 1966.

** Then M.P. for Kidderminster. Subsequently knighted. Retired at General Election, 1964. M.P. for South Worcestershire, 1966.

Tory backbenchers to whom I have already referred as the Woolton recruits of the late 1940s. They were those who had joined up, like myself, 'to set the people free' and who now, at various stages of their middle-age, formed a corps of like-thinking people in the Conservative Parliamentary Party, faithful to the middle-class way of life and the libertarian way of thinking of their own political generation. Worthy people indeed, despite their faults—the principal one of which was their over-readiness to fit in with a scheme of things which called upon them to serve in a subservient capacity to those of greater social distinction, but of inferior brain power, and to accept an interpretation of that much-abused word 'loyalty' which could ill stand the strain of analysis. But analysis in any form has never been a strong feature of the Conservative Party.

None the less, the main body of these people, the heavily billed 'Tory backbenchers' of the Press during these years, by and large took it ill that they were the helpless spectators of wholesale ministerial surrenders to socialism, whether it be to Socialist theory, to open Opposition pressure or to Government department ukase. Reinforced as they were by the intake of the 1955 Election, when the fresh series of Conservative victories in the industrial and surburban 'marginals' had brought in a number of like-minded characters, they represented a considerable body of opinion who endeavoured to set their faces against the compromise between the Conservative leadership and socialism, which they saw going on day by day before their eyes.

Gerald Nabarro had made himself a rallying point of this disaffection by his onslaught on the Government's tireless financing of the losses of the National Coal Board. This was a cleverly chosen battleground which, attacking the enemy at his weakest point, had yielded several tactical successes.

A skilful parliamentary general, Gerald had led his troops into the lobby for more than one vote against the Government and, though this was inevitably a harmless gesture inasmuch as the chosen issue was one on which the Labour Party was bound to abstain (or, indeed, support the Government), it formed a medium of protest for those who were unhappy about the general drift of surrender to Socialist policies. Thus, on 10th May 1956 he mustered some twenty active 'rebel' voting supporters against the Coal Industry Bill; and more than that on a subsequent occasion. While even many of those whose sense of dedication to the Party did not allow them to enter the Nabarro lobby obtained some vicarious satisfaction from his activities.

Gerald has, since then, established himself as a political prophet to the nation, but on this particular occasion it was I, and not he, who was in prophetic mood. The prospects of our 'rebel' lobby were, I seem to remember saying, of the very brightest. Opinion Polls, even in June 1959, were forecasting the third Tory General Election victory with a further fifty seats. These seats, so I argued, as we sat on the sundeck of m.v. *Kronprincesse Ingrid* the following morning, would bring in the same type of Member as had the marginals which had been won in 1955, the traditionally-minded middle-aged professional and business types, who would automatically recruit to our lobby. It was merely a matter of time before the trend of continual surrender to socialism could be reversed.

Seldom have I been more wrong. Within a few months the Party did, indeed, win its fifty extra seats, but the names of those associated with the victories in the 1959 Election— Julian Crichley* (Rochester and Chatham), Peter Tapsell* (South Nottingham), Humphry Berkeley* (Lancaster), Charles Longbottom* (York), twelve members of the Bow Group (so it was said—even though not all the *soidisant* Bow Groupers were identifiable by the Bow Group itself)—were no supporters for the Nabarro lobby. Indeed, I cannot recollect that my poor friend, Gerald, gained a single recruit.

The Tories for Progress had arrived at Westminster! Then, with these protagonists in the van, yapping joyfully and frolicking in their wake, with encouraging pats on the back from Mr. Harold Macmillan, there was the Bow Group itself—this gifted group of junior politicians whose pro-

* These four gentlemen were defeated at the 1964 and 1966 General Elections. Mr. Peter Tapsell, after being defeated in South Nottingham in 1964, was elected M.P. for Holland and Boston Division in Lincolnshire of 1966.

nouncements suddenly, from 1959 onwards, carried Delphic authority with both Press and Prime Minister.

To anyone such as myself, who perhaps fancied himself as a senior oracle following twenty-five years in the business, it was somewhat bewildering that here was an oracle of such greater virtue, sprung, as it were, like Athene out of the head of Zeus, without any of the pains of gestation: I have had to console myself with the vicarious satisfaction that the next generation of the Johnson family, Anne, my daughter-in-law (Literary Editor of *Crossbow*) and Christopher (a frequent contributor to this magazine), played an integral part in this revelation.

It was by no means easy, in the midst of a crowded life, to comprehend straightaway that here was a fresh political phenomenon which, engineered by changes in the Conservative Central Office the significance of which went unnoticed at the time, was to turn upside down the whole traditional set-up of the Conservative Party. Even so explicit a statement as that of Lord Hailsham in January 1959, which I quoted at the beginning of Chapter Four, was not recognised as presaging the elimination of an entire generation from the Conservative parliamentary candidature lists and the wholesale adoption of younger people in their twenties and thirties, with its consequent effect on the composition of the parliamentary Party in the years to come—and, of course, its pattern of behaviour in addition.

It goes without saying that, in contrast to this glorification of the younger and 'progressive' generation, the influence of the older and more 'reactionary' rebels waned. Gerald Nabarro's rebel vote had dropped to thirteen when he called a Division on the Coal Industry Bill on 27th January 1960, while on Schedule A (a matter of far wider interest than Coal Nationalisation) on 22nd June of that year, he could only get a mere eight supporters into his dissident lobby. The Nabarro lobby had ceased to be a parliamentary force and Gerald's remaining time in this Parliament (rudely interrupted by illness) was marked entirely by his brilliant, though highly individual, campaign against purchase tax.

Indeed, there were no more votes against the Macmillan Government called by any Conservative parliamentary rebel, except perhaps, if it can be qualified as such, my own unofficial vote on 14th February 1962 on my Private Member's Ten-Minute Rule Bill on the subject of Compulsory Vaccination when, against the recommendation of the Government Whips, with my colleagues, Harold Gurden* and Raymond Gower,** as my tellers, I obtained seventy-seven supporters: a number unequalled even by my friend, Gerald.

By the early 1960s the drive towards a 'progressive' Britain —a Britain of diminished liberty and personal independence at home and the abandonment of Imperial mission abroad— all under the aegis of Mr. Harold Macmillan—could not be gainsaid. Tory backbenchers who still attempted to stay this process were but a rump, reduced to grumblings on Party Committees, occasional protests in the debating Chamber or sour letters to the Press, of which less than no notice was taken by those who controlled the levers of power.

Though this discontent of the Tory backbenchers had in the late 1950s undoubtedly gained much sympathy in the country, particularly amongst those sections of the middle classes from which they had themselves sprung, this dissipated itself in the light of the recurring exposure of their ineffectiveness.

'Tory backbenchers mostly burn as weakly as poor quality firelighters,' stated the *Sunday Times* commentary at the time of the dispute with Mr. Peter Thorneycroft over the Skybolt deal and the Nassau meeting. 'But' continues that paper, 'in the public mind irritable bewilderment lingers on.'

These brief sentences indicate the situation over the wider front.

* * * * *

But what could be done? The answer was, so it seemed, 'nothing'.

'TORY REVOLT' screamed the headlines, week after

* Harold Gurden, Conservative M.P. for Selly Oak Division of Birmingham.
** Raymond Gower, Conservative M.P. for Barry (South Wales).

week—over the nationalised coal industry, over drugs for private patients, over the loans to nationalised industries, over the surrender to trade union demands, over Africa, over Schedule A taxation—to name but a few of the leading issues —until it seemed over the years of the 1959–64 Parliament that the real struggle in this Parliament was no longer between the two Front Benches, but between the Government Front Bench, supported by the Labour Opposition, on the one hand, and the Tory backbenchers on the other—the first two being in a permanently victorious alliance over the third party. In these circumstances revolt after revolt was quelled with the same speed and efficiency as similar emotional outbreaks in institutions of an even more penal nature than the House of Commons.

Added to feelings of frustration were feelings of betrayal. One hundred and eighty backbenchers, practically the whole of the non-ministerial strength of the Parliamentary Tory Party, signed a Motion on the Order Paper in favour of private patients being given the facility for obtaining drugs under the National Health Service, in accordance with the pre-election pledge of the Conservative Party prior to 1950. But nothing happened and, after all, where did you go from here?

From home affairs, let us look at wider horizons overseas. Seventy to eighty of these same people signed another Motion concerning the Central African Federation. In this latter instance accusations of personal betrayal were added to those of political betrayal inasmuch as Sir Roy Welensky (as he has since revealed in his memoirs) was heard to complain that, in 1960, when Mr. Robin Turton* and others were protesting in the House against Mr. Macmillan's 'Wind of Change' policy in Africa, Dr. Hastings Banda, at that time in prison as an insurgent, was being visited by the Socialist M.P., Mr. Dingle Foot, Q.C., on 23rd and 24th January as an emissary from the British Conservative Government.

But, though Robin Turton pleaded diligently and per-

* The Right Hon. Robert Turton, Conservative M.P. for Thirsk and Maldon (Yorkshire), Minister of Health, 1956–57.

sistently in his opposition to 'the Wind of Change', he was no Winston Churchill, any more than had been his predecessor who led the Suez rebels, Captain Charles Waterhouse. Nor was he a Gerald Nabarro, to embarrass the Government by calling a vote against them.

As I sat on the benches throughout the Africa debates, I could not help but recall that day some thirty or more years previously, back in the distant 1920s, when, a young medical student imbued with radical ideas, I had joined the small crowd gathered round a local Conservative Junior Imperial League speaker in the High Street of the pleasant town of Berkhamsted, Hertfordshire (where I was lodging at the time), and I had presumed to heckle some particularly platitudinous statement.

I had suddenly found a fist near my nose and a threatening voice in my ear:

'Do you believe in the British Empire?'

The eyes of a hostile crowd were turned on me. If I had not said a quick 'Yes', I do not know what the outcome of this encounter might have been.

But here, thirty years later, I was witness of the entire British Empire being parcelled out by a Conservative Prime Minister like gifts at a tombola session—without a single effective protest, without so much as a vote being called in the House of Commons. While, as for the Conservative Associations, those formidable bodies, still wrapped in their Union Jacks, still intoning 'Land of Hope and Glory' (albeit not so loudly and frequently as at one time), still with their slogans of Queen and Empire (now changed to 'our great Elizabethan Commonwealth'), were discarding the Mission which they had cherished for so long, abandoning the British settlers in African countries to a sorrowful fate.

As if held in thrall by a strange hypnotic force, the great Tory elephant slowly, gradually, stood on its head at the behest of its expert ringmaster—Harold Macmillan.

*   *   *   *   *

Where does the power lie?

Few people are so ill-informed as to believe any longer that it lies in the lobbies of the House of Commons. With the extension of bureaucracy in the modern State, power—constructive power, that is, the power to create policy and to carry out decisions, lies elsewhere, inside the apparatus of government. Behind the scenes and beyond the public eye. The *Sunday Times* in its excellent leading article 'Power and the Press' in its issue of 21st February 1965, explains why it had decided on the innovation of appointing its 'Whitehall Correspondent'.

'There can be no doubt where power has flown' states the *Sunday Times*. 'For the last fifty years Parliament has become steadily weaker. Decisions are not now taken in Parliament: they are not often taken in Cabinet. They are frequently taken in the Ministries, by negotiations between Ministries and in negotiations between Ministries and outside interests. . . . Power has gone to the departments and, wherever power goes, it is the job of the journalist to follow and to inform. . . . Real power often tries to hide its hand, and to leave mock power to appear to exercise its functions. As a newspaper the *Sunday Times* is still going to report real power and not merely maintain the pretence that Parliament decides everything.'

Hurrah for the *Sunday Times*!

What would its Whitehall Correspondent have found in his search for real power during the days of the Government of Mr. Macmillan? He would have found Lord Robens (ex-Socialist M.P.) at the Coal Board, Sir Geoffrey de Freitas (ex-Socialist M.P.) at key official posts in Africa first in Ghana and then Kenya, Mr. Chetwynd (ex-Socialist M.P.) as Chairman of the North-East Development Council. In the Church he would have found the Reverend Mervyn Stockwood, formerly a protagonist of Sir Richard Acland's Commonwealth Party, appointed Bishop of Southwark. In and around the Ministries he would have found Sir Solly Zuckerman as Scientific Adviser of Defence; and, coming to the newly ennobled, he would have found that few people counted more in health politics than Lord Taylor (formerly Dr. Stephen Taylor, Socialist M.P. for Barnet), or in welfare state economics than Baroness Wootton, the well-known Fabian.

All these were creations of Mr. Harold Macmillan **as** Prime Minister—and one could well ask were the Conservatives in power, or were they only in mock power, wandering in futile protest around the lobbies of the House of Commons? For our hypothetical Whitehall Correspondent would have sought in vain to find any equivalent body of Conservatives thus honoured—apart, that is, from an occasional Old Etonian High Commissioner and Colonial Governor. (Paradoxically enough, it had to await the accession of Labour Government before any Conservative politician—Conservative politician of humble origin anyway—was, in the person of Mr. Aubrey Jones, to compete in any place of real power.)

The names which I have mentioned did not, admittedly, shine as brightly as the constellation of Conservative Ministers, who had come to power and held their proud positions through virtue of service to the Conservative Party. But it was only a matter of time before these latter suffered the reverse fate. For, as we all know, there came the week-end in June 1963 when an entire galaxy of political stars, the leaders of that sad generation of Conservatives of whom I have been talking, struck by the Jovian thunderbolts of the Prime Minister's demand for their resignations, fell unprotestingly from the sky, leaving a gap in the political firmament as if they had never existed and the Conservative Party for all the world looking like the final scene of a Shakespearian melodrama, the stage littered with the political corpses of those who had had their day, even though still in their middle and late fifties.

So was the scene set for the entry of the Young Fortinbras— the future generation—the young and progressive Tory— those 'not too rigid and set in their ways' and who were uninhibited by outmoded aspirations and out-of-date ideas, who would give the Party its new image and lead it to victory.

So it might have been, but for the Profumo affair which we shall be studying in this book and the notoriously perversity of the British electorate, who evidently considered that, if they were to have socialism anyway, they might as well have the real thing in Harold Wilson.

CHAPTER SIX

ENNUI AT WESTMINSTER

THERE WAS an immense buzz up and down the lobbies at Westminster on 17th March 1960. The 'school' was in a fair tizzy.

What had happened to Ted Heath? Was he crackers? Had he been overworking? Had you seen *The Times*?

The consternation was understandable, for this is the report from the centre page of *The Times* of that date:

WASTING TIME IN PARLIAMENT

MR. HEATH ON ENNUI IN THE COMMONS

Mr. Edward Heath, Minister of Labour, complained last night of the 'woeful waste of time' in the House of Commons.

Mr. Heath, who was speaking at a meeting of the Conservative Political Centre at Church House, Westminster, said that there were terribly protracted debates on the Second Reading of Bills.

'The Committee Stage of a Bill you have really mastered' he said, 'is interesting and instructive, but even this stage is too protracted, and then comes a later stage—the Report Stage—when a great deal is said all over again; and even this is frequently followed by a debate on the Third Reading.

AIR OF LANGUOR

'Of course, you are not in the House all the time. There are the library, the tea room and the smoking room, where you may play Chess or Draughts but no other

72

game whatsoever. But nobody does anything vehemently. An air of languor pervades the whole place. Listlessness abounds. Members stroll from one room to another, turn over the newspapers and yawn in each other's faces.

'In the summer from five o'clock to seven the terrace is crowded with fine ladies and country cousins, drinking tea and devouring strawberries. Occasionally some parliamentary person of importance will choose to stalk by, and even—such is the affability of true greatness— have a cup of tea with a party of friends. A poorer way of killing time has not, I think, been discovered: but it is convincing proof of the *ennui* of parliamentary life.'

It so happened that on that same afternoon—and you may reckon this as one of my recurring coincidences—I had a Question down for the Prime Minister about the possible employment of Members of Parliament on Royal Commissions and it was accordingly irresistible, in my 'supplementary', to bring in some mention of *ennui*—a very real phenomenon as far as I was concerned by this time after five years in Parliament.

The explanation was that the Minister, in his talk that was reported, had been quoting from the address by Augustine Birrell to the Cowdenbeath Literary Society on 15th October 1896.

Ted Heath, happy himself in his work at the House of Commons, had been quoting this extract with a view to contrasting the atmosphere of the 1890s to the busy hive of contented workers when he evidently saw, or imagined that he saw, through his own rose-tinted spectacles, at time of speaking. But others saw the scene differently. Indeed, it must be considered a tribute to the static qualities of the Honourable House that a talk given in 1896 can, some sixty-five years later, be mistaken for a picture of the contemporary scene.

But was there *ennui* at Westminster? There was indeed: and six years later again, as this is written, a new generation of (Labour) Government backbenchers are howling with the agony of it. It must inevitably be thus when so little opportunity for constructive work is available to Members, the majority of whom do not share the fruits of office and who are only too painfully aware that all decisions of importance are taken over their heads. It is an *ennui* punctuated only by the semi-schoolboy disturbances in the House which provide the occasion for contemporary criticism, such as that of Mr. David Butler in the *Sunday Times* of 25th April 1965, when he declared them to 'excite uncomprehending and bored contempt in the world outside Westminster'; or by the occasional exasperated protest such as that of Mr. Geoffrey Hirst, Conservative M.P. for Shipley, at the 'disgraceful treatment' accorded to Conservative backbenchers in Mr. Heath's refusal to produce a White Paper in advance of the Resale Prices Bill in 1964. It is an *ennui* intensified by the consciousness that it is just those who have devoted their life to the practice of politics and political study, who at the peak of their powers are now deprived of all share in the construction of policy. Not unnaturally they consider themselves the victims of an unfair and absurd situation.

I must say it again. It is the essence of the M.P.s' frustration that Parliament, though the historic law-making body, has let its powers slip so far that, with the exception of the occasional Private Member's Bill dealing with some non-political matter, the framing of legislation and the formulation of policy that produces the legislation has passed over entirely to the Executive—the Government and its civil service. While the role of Parliament is reduced to that of ineffective protest.

The genesis of policy has passed away from the open political assemblies. The sound and fury of the 'ginger groups' counts for little in comparison with the quiet determination of a single well-placed civil servant; while exploration of policy issues has passed to those mysterious and recondite bodies, the Royal Commissions and the Departmental Committees of Inquiries into problems of every variety, which have proliferated so vastly in recent times.

It was the small part played by elected Members of Parliament in these bodies which led to my asking the Prime Minister in the House on 17th March 1960—the day to which

I have already referred in the first part of this chapter—'if he would give instructions to Ministers that they should ask a larger number of M.P.s to serve on such Commissions and Inquiries'.*

This was the answer which I received:

The Prime Minister: 'I think it is best to maintain the utmost flexibility in this matter, since the aim must always be to secure the services of those best qualified to take part. There are, of course, occasions when the understanding and experience of hon. Members qualifies them particularly for appointment to Royal Commissions and Committees of Inquiry; and I am sure that this is a factor which Ministers do not overlook.'

Mr. Macmillan vouchsafed no definition as to who was best qualified. That hon. Members of Parliament did not 'qualify' very often was clear from the figures which I now quote from a written answer which he had given to me a few days previously. This stated that, out of 667 members of some 70 Royal Commissions and Committees of Inquiry appointed over the previous five years, only 16 M.P.s had, in fact, been appointed. (I was told, incidentally, that the answering of this Question threw the Prime Minister's office out of gear for about a fortnight.)

* * * * *

What I have said so far in this chapter is applicable to all M.P.s, but it is the back-bench Government M.P. who finds himself in a particularly invidious position.

In the first place, the sister of ineffectiveness for the back-bench Government M.P. is uncertainty. This uncertainty is of a twofold nature. Uncertainty as to his prospects of promotion at the hands of his Party hierarchy, and uncertainty as to his fate at the hands of the electors, particularly if he happens to represent a marginal seat. As I have indicated in Chapter Three, he is left to form such opinion as to his parliamentary prospects as he sees fit and he is not to be blamed if, as the

* *Hansard*: Vol. 619, Columns 1474, 1475.

years go by uneventfully, he begins to take a lugubrious view. But he cannot keep his gaze on these alone, for in the other direction there is the swing of the electoral pendulum to be watched, carrying with it the threat of electoral defeat and possible political elimination. This inevitably makes him think of his future in a more personal light, as, if he is a reasonably prudent person, he must have continually under review his prospects of making a living outside Parliament in event of electoral defeat.

As he does this, he is already half-way along the road to political ruin. For, regardless of these considerations, the Party does not cease to demand single-minded 100 per cent loyalty as the price of its favours, however minor these may be.

Let us examine 'Party loyalty'—that all-demanding entity.

It is now three-quarters of a century since W. S. Gilbert wrote the song of Private Willis in *Iolanthe*:

> ' When in that House M.P.'s divide
> If they've a brain and cerebellum too,
> They've got to leave that brain outside
> And vote just as their leaders tell 'em to.'

Since then society has become more complex, the authority of Whitehall has expanded and the powers of civil servants have proliferated, but Parliament with its time-honoured customs has remained static. Despite the higher calibre of intelligence of the individual Member, it is still resented if he does not leave the analytical part of his brain on the peg in the Members' Cloak Room, with the small piece of pink ribbon that was originally intended for Members' swords.

Who can wonder at the decline in status of M.P.s which is so frequently the occasion for comment?

It can be that there are other reasons for the onset of *ennui* amongst back-bench M.P.s beyond even the frustration, the long hours of imprisonment at the call of the Party Whip, the crowded premises and the close atmosphere.

Why are there so few scientists in the House of Commons?

It is surely that those who have been taught to observe

facts, to evaluate evidence in a dispassionate manner, to form
conclusions untainted by preconceived notions, and to view
any situation with critical appreciation, find a company in
which almost every question is judged predominantly by
extraneous considerations of 'Party loyalty' to be one in which
they find difficulty in adapting themselves.

It may well be that the Minister—to whom, let it be remembered, you owe unswerving loyalty—has been caught out
implementing a perverse decision taken by the civil servants
of his Department, or alternatively he may be defending
some conspicuous error of theirs. He will, with his reputation
at stake, be declaring that such and such a decision, or such
and such an error, is white, while all objective considerations
show that it is black, as black as black can be. Maybe the
Opposition has seized on this and, even though the point at
issue has no identifiable political context, it is soon a question
of confidence. This is the time for all good men to come to the
aid of the Party. Do you have the temerity to continue to
declare that black is not white, but is conspicuously black?
Then you are a traitor to the Party, whose collective duty
it is to defend the Minister in all circumstances, whatever
either he or his subordinates have done.

So, in an age of scientific enlightenment, does Parliament
disacculturate itself from all objective processes of thought and
conduct its affairs on an emotional basis reminiscent of earlier
times.

It is difficult enough when this occurs occasionally in
individual cases, but, in the years between 1955 and 1964
this was the predicament in which the main body of the
Conservative Parliamentary Party found itself. It was soon
clear that it was one thing for a Party to come back to power
on a finite policy such as that described by *The Financial Times*
correspondent—'economic progress and expansion in freedom,
decontrol and a new chance for the individual after a period
of collectivism': but it was another thing to implement this
policy throughout the years.

The Ministers of the appropriate Departments had the
responsibility of deciding the interpretation of policy and, so

often during these years being clueless people anyway, lacking detailed knowledge and study of their problems in advance, they were utterly dependent on their advisers—the permanent civil service heads of the Departments. It was not surprising that what emerged was, on occasions, totally unrecognisable as Conservative policy. Thus the recurrent situations, worthy of the pen of another W. S. Gilbert, whereby Party discipline, and appeals to Party loyalty, were used directly to defeat the policies to which the Party was pledged to the electorate.

The choice of the Government backbencher in the face of this was between complete subservience on the one hand, or ineffective protest on the other—protest, of course, against a Government which he nominally supported, with all the strains and the conflicts of loyalty that were thereby involved. One might defy the subtle pressures and take advantage of one's prerogative of free speech, but if the Party Whips were against you, whispering here and whispering there, free and open speech was of little use, whether on Party Committees or on the floor of the Debating Chamber itself. For instance, pursuit of a special cause by an amendment to current legislation could only lead perhaps to the ultimate absurdity of a Government Member being expected to vote against his own amendment which perhaps five minutes previously he had been sponsoring with fervour. (It was one of the most mischievous tricks of the Opposition during those years that they were prone to 'call', i.e. insist on a vote on, such amendments as this when the embarrassed sponsor was anxious to withdraw both himself and his amendment from the scene.)

*   *   *   *   *

But why go on? Everything that I now write about is general knowledge and discussed over and over again by the Sunday columnists and other political correspondents. An attack on the Whips—on whose unfortunate head the stupidity of the system is personalised—is a good headline in almost any paper.

But nobody does anything about it. No Government has

shewn any tendency to make it less easy for itself to govern:
Opposition Leaders likewise are not going to make the leadership of their party more difficult. Beyond that, protests are of
a sporadic and ineffective nature. The electorate, oblivious to
the fact that it is losing its own liberties, approves rather than
otherwise of its politicians being put into strait-jackets.

Meanwhile, slowly, the life blood drains away from the
House of Commons (in the same way as we will see it draining
away from the British medical profession in my next chapter),
as one experienced and intelligent Member after the other
decides that there is no place for him and quietly takes his
leave.

Party loyalty, or at least the further prospects in life
dependent so often on the continued goodwill of the Party,
demands discretion on such occasions. Only now and then does
a comment show itself—as, for instance, on the retirement of
Mr. P. B. Lucas, Conservative M.P. for Brentford and Chis-
wick, R.A.F. fighter ace and former Captain of the British
Walker Cup team, prior to the 1959 Election, we find the
political correspondent of the *Daily Telegraph* lamenting thus:
'There are now nearly 30 Conservative M.P.s who have
announced their intention not to stand again and possibly
a good many others who have privately taken the same
decision. Most of these are elderly, but Mr. Lucas at 43 is
in the age-group of M.P.s on whom both Parties must build
for the future.'

We owe much therefore to one of those assiduous American
researchers, Professor Philip W. Buck of Stanford University
who, in his interesting book, *Amateurs and Professionals in British
Politics*,* has analysed a whole section of opinion which he
defines as that of 'a number of people who had won and held
seats in the House of Commons who decided to withdraw
from politics when they might have continued'.

Professor Buck identified a total of 150 ex-Members as
leaving during the years 1918 to 1959 and he was able to
elicit detailed replies as to their reasons for doing this from

* *Amateurs and Professionals in British Politics*, by Philip W. Buck (University of
Chicago Press, 70 Great Russell St., London, W.C.1), pp. 67, 124.

no less than 82 of these people. In this he has done a considerable service in penetrating the façade of the polite excuses that are the customary feature of the withdrawal of so many of my former colleagues. The 'business reasons', the 'family reasons' and the 'health reasons' which gloss over a situation in which any other form of announcement would only 'let the Party down' and, incidentally, perhaps interfere with any well-deserved future recognition of services rendered.

Professor Buck has set out his answers in the form of percentages as follows:

1. Circumstances force a choice between profession or business and continuing in politics. (For about two-fifths of these this was also combined with financial sacrifice)   32 per cent
2. Health reasons   ..   ..   23 per cent
3. Politics not satisfactory for realisation of goals of public service as formulated in personal judgment ..   ..   17 per cent
4. Dissatisfaction with Party programme or Party discipline   ..   ..   12 per cent
5. Personal and family reasons   ..   ..   8 per cent
6. Financial sacrifice ..   ..   4 per cent
7. Unable to secure adoption as a candidate..   4 per cent

The business reasons, the health reasons and the family reasons are not absent from the above schedule. On the other hand, here are almost one-third of those retiring admitting privately that parliamentary politics is a disappointing pastime and that parliamentary life is too irksome for them to pursue.

'All had been able and energetic members of the House of Commons', states Professor Buck, 'and had been successful in elections . . . their decision to withdraw must be regarded as a loss to politics of their energy, ability and accumulated experience.'

These researches must, in the nature of things, substantially apply to backbenchers of the Government Party: if so, the words of Professor Buck sounded the death-knell of the Conservative Party in Parliament.

'Loyalty is the Conservative Party's secret weapon,' declared the Earl of Kilmuir in his memoirs. But loyalty—the code of exaggerated obligation by which a man was expected to sacrifice himself silently in the face of outrage and injustice—was also an infernal machine ticking away until the final cataclysm took place with the breakdown of Party morale in 1963. Relentlessly, the individual grievances and the humiliations accumulated to lead first to a schism between backbenchers and Ministers, then in due course to the disastrous state of affairs between backbenchers and the Prime Minister in the summer of 1963—of which I shall have to write. Each individual disgruntlement may not have counted for much at the time it occurred, but a long succession of these created a cumulative sourness and sense of boredom which seeped through the Party as a whole with disastrous results.

But I cannot do better than illustrate what I have said with a brief account of my own experiences in the sphere in which I have some claim to special interest.

CHAPTER SEVEN

THE SICKNESS OF THE SACRED COW

'Twas a Winter's night in London,
And as cold as the hinside of a 'fridge,
And the National 'Ealth Scheme's Last G.P.,
Was a-jumping off Westminster Bridge.
But dinin' in style in the Commons,
Hin their 'igh and himperious pride,
The Cabinet saw 'is intention,
And one and all of them cried,

'Don't jump in the river, dear Doctor,
You're all the G.P. that we've got!
Consider us chaps should the 'Ealth Scheme collapse,
Why you'd probably get us all shot!
'As something hoccurred to upset you?
We'll 'asten to 'ave it put right!
But the 'ole of our mob'll be out of a job
If you jump in the river to-night!'

The Lancet: *In England Now*

THERE CAN be no dispute that, in the story of the Welfare
State in Britain thus far, the sphere of maximum failure
has been in the Government's dealings with the doctors
—in particular with the 'family doctors', thus called in
accordance with Ministry of Health and Press jargon to
designate the general practitioners of medicine.

The strife and disaster in this section of the National Health
Service are now too familiar to need description: and that
they are the deep responsibility of the administrators of the

Ministry of Health and the obstinacy with which they have conducted their affairs must likewise be accepted. For they cannot say that they were not warned. Long, long before 'What is Really Wrong with Our Health Services' became the popular headline that it is to-day, I warned them myself.

The proposition is a simple one, but it is yet to be appreciated by the British public. You cannot run a Health Service without doctors: it is not the politicians, nor the civil servants, who get up in the middle of the night to respond to the call for help. The treatment of doctors since the commencement of the National Health Service has come very close to what is euphemistically termed 'civilian conscription in peacetime'. Over the whole of the time about which I have been writing, no attempt whatsoever was made to listen to the professional views of doctors concerning their conditions of work. In increasing numbers, therefore, from the early 1950s onwards, doctors have started to emigrate to the United States and countries within the White Commonwealth, where such conditions are more congenial—and, incidentally, pay is better. This problem was ignored over the years, as a result of which the movement has gathered momentum until to-day it appears to be the established pattern in a free society that a substantial proportion of our younger doctors emigrate. To-day the very existence of the National Health Service is threatened owing to lack of medical manpower.

It cannot on this occasion be counted a coincidence that this breakdown has occurred in a sphere in which, over the almost twenty years since the inception of the National Health Service under the Act of 1946,* we have seen a Government Department relentlessly pursuing a policy of its own, ignoring statistical facts, bending even the sternest of Ministers to its will, first brushing aside and then finally breaking any politician so foolhardy to oppose it.

There is, in fact, no other Department of State that can illustrate the contentions of my previous chapters (which also find confirmation throughout Reginald Bevins' book, *The*

* The 'appointed day' for the National Health Service Act, 1946, was 4th July 1948. The service started, therefore, two years after the Act.

Greasy Pole) better than the Ministry of Health. A *parvenu* Ministry, established in its present importance in our national life only since the extended powers endowed on it by the National Health Service Act 1946, it has little truck with archaic ideas of parliamentary democracy and individual freedom. 'Modern' and 'with it' politically, if not otherwise, it runs its affairs as a benevolent autocracy, ignoring all opinion that may emanate from anywhere outside its ivory tower at the Elephant and Castle (or Number 23 Savile Row, as it was in my day in Parliament). Reacting in antagonistic fashion to all criticism, the Ministry of Health is the spoilt child of bureaucracy in as much as, until very recent days, it has enjoyed total protection owing to the 'sacred cow' attitude of the general public towards the National Health Service. Thus even Parliamentary Questions, so great a terror to other departments (or, at least, allegedly so) with their specially labelled files can cheerfully be used in contemptuous fashion as spills for lighting the pipes of desk-bound doctors at the Ministry. In this Service Parliament has, indeed, a Franken-stein monster on its hands, which it can neither control nor rid itself of.

In *The British General Election of 1964* Mr. David Butler speculates, in the course of his comments on M.P.s and the Election, why it was that I was a casualty before going to the polls in failing to secure re-nomination by my local Party in Carlisle, while many others of my colleagues, equally rebellious, suffered no harm. I can inform him that the primary reason for this was my ill luck in that, as a doctor M.P., this was the Department with which I clashed in what I felt to be the proper course of my public duty in taking interest in health matters in the House of Commons.

Other medical and parliamentary colleagues, on the Conservative side of the House anyway, took the more circum-spect course of giving the Health Service a fairly wide berth and finding scope for their talents in other spheres.

Far from condemning them for this, I must commend them for their prudence, for I was to pay a heavy price for my own idiosyncratic course. Indeed my political epitaph might well be a parallel quotation to that which, I am told, can be found on a gravestone in a Cheltenham churchyard:

> Here lie I and my three daughters
>   Who died of drinking Cheltenham waters
> If we had kept to Epsom Salts
>   We wouldn't be lying in these 'ere vaults.

What then was the occasion for my conflict with the Ministry of Health—and, of course, successive Ministers?

'Surely one feels that "a national plan" must be something willed by all of us and good for all of us? But the reality which this abstraction, "the State", conceals is something very different. Lift the curtain and "the State" reveals itself as a little group of fallible men in Whitehall, making guesses about the future, influenced by political pressures and partisan prejudices and working on projections drawn from the past by a staff of economists.

'Of a "national plan" thus produced we can assert three things in confidence. It is likely to be wrong, dead wrong, in its major conceptions; its errors will do the maximum damage because they will be imposed on the whole economy; and they will be persisted in long after they have been revealed, because governments are the slowest of all creatures to admit themselves mistaken and a State plan, of all plans, is the most inflexible.'*

Thus spake Enoch the Evangelist. Enoch Powell did not say these words specifically about the Department of which, until a few days previously, he had been the Head. But, whether he meant them to apply or not, they can certainly be applied to the Ministry of Health and were, as I shall show, the very basis of my objection to this arrogant Department. In the meantime, in the course of this demonstration, we shall be encountering another character—yet another Enoch. This time it is Enoch, the Minister, to all outward appearance identical with the first Enoch, but whose attitude of mind and the content of whose speech were as different under the alternating situations of freedom and office, as have been that

* Mr. Enoch Powell speaking at Bromley on Thursday, 2nd October 1963.

of the Conservative Party as a whole. It was as if the dichotomy of thought and action which afflicts the Party, according to whether it is operating in the freedom of opposition or in office, became epitomised in one man. There are doubtless explanations for this: but these cannot be my concern. I merely state the facts of the political drama in which I took a part.

For, of course, the Conservative Party, which—when in Opposition—phrased and paraphrased the words of Mr. Enoch Powell (Enoch the Evangelist, that is) in thousands of leaflets and pamphlets and on an equal number of platforms throughout the country, showed itself to be ineffective and bankrupt of policy when it came to dealing as a Government with a centralised organisation. As a consequence, the National Health Service was left totally unchanged throughout thirteen years of Conservative Government without one single amendment in any important particular, whether as a concession to Conservative thought or even as a sop to changing times, still less in response to the representations of any professional organisation.

In surveying the political course of the Conservative Government during its time in charge of the Welfare State, it is understandable, if not necessarily laudable, that, in accordance with the Japanese proverb that 'the wise bamboo bends before the gale', the hierarchy should compromise as best it could with the tidal wave of socialism that had swept the country in the immediate post-war years, but, as the electors moved gradually rightwards in their allegiance, there was less and less excuse for this. Indeed, in the light of the substantial Conservative majority at the 1959 Election and the fact that the jerry-built structure of the National Health Service had already started to creak at the joints from its many imperfections, it became more and more openly a breach of faith with its supporters that Conservative Government made no attempt to modify this Service in fulfilment of its election pledges.

This was the situation at the beginning of the 1959 Parliament. While, on the other hand, here I was, once again established as a Member of Parliament for a second term, looking for a fresh mission, and, at least, with the advantage of comprehensive experience in the various branches of the Health Service, whether it be general practice, hospital work, administration or even the educational side.

But, in my endeavour to reform the National Health Service, I soon found that, as I charged forward to engage the foe, so did my target recede. My re-election to Parliament was in October 1959 and I find that it was seven months later, on 5th May 1960, that, somewhat impatiently perhaps, I am asking Mr. R. A. Butler, Leader of the House, 'whether he can find time for a general debate on the National Health Service? Is he aware that there are problems of very considerable importance accumulating in this Service, particularly relevant to the general practitioners, rightly described as the basis of the Service? So far we have not had this Session a general debate on this Service which is costing the country £700 million or more a year.'

'I think that my hon. friend's request is reasonable,' replied Mr. R. A. Butler. 'It is simply a question of finding the time.'*

But the answer to this question was in the negative. At least, until a half-day Debate on Supplementary Estimates in the next Session of Parliament on 6th December 1960. A whole year had gone by during which there had been no possibility of debating the National Health Service at all.

This was the first obstacle to my making any impression on the National Health Service as a doctor in Parliament. In the brave apocalyptic era of the late 1940s, when the parliamentary machine was working under pressure in transforming 'faith into works' in the Socialist revelation, many things were inevitably overlooked. One of the most important of these matters that escaped attention was the provision of any means by which Parliament could keep control over the monster to which it had given birth.

Whereas in the case of the older spending Departments, such as the Treasury (in the Finance Debates), the Defence Departments (in the annual debates on Army, Navy and Air

* *Hansard*: Vol. 622, Column 1263.

Force Estimates), parliamentary supervision is jealously retained by the allotted provision for debates written into the parliamentary programme, in this new and more freely spending age no such precaution was taken in the setting up of a Service which was quickly to vie with all others in its costliness. I am not aware that any suggestion was made to remedy this defect, even by the Conservative Party in Opposition to the Bill in the 1940s—or subsequently in Government. Indeed the Conservative Government was so engaged in covering its shame at ever having criticised the National Health Service Bill at all, that this basic precaution of sound finance and parliamentary accountability was not mooted at any time.

Thus, in the 1959–64 Parliament—or in any other Parliament —the Service had to compete for space in an already over-crowded parliamentary programme and such attention as it obtained depended entirely on the whims of either Government or Opposition Parties: neither of which, for their own separate reasons—the former as carrying the responsibility for the efficiency of its administration, the latter on account of its traditional attitude to 'the sacred cow'—was anxious during the late 1950s and early sixties to have its shortcomings receive too much ventilation.

Inevitably, therefore, the opportunities for M.P.s to express their views on the Service in Parliament, and so influence its development, are highly capricious in their occurrence. Nothing could be more illustrative of this than the course of events in the three annual Sessions between October 1959 and August 1962. For, after there being only one half-day Debate in fifteen months, Parliamentary interest in the Health Service suddenly sprang to life with the National Health Services Contributions Bill, introduced on 15th February 1961, whereby Mr. Enoch Powell (Enoch the Minister) proposed to raise the prescription charge from 1s to 2s, and the National Health Insurance Contribution by 1s per week.

This was regarded by the Labour Opposition as too good a political opportunity to miss. MORE MIDNIGHT ANGER AT WELFARE STATE 'ASSAULT' runs a contemporary headline above a description of one of the late-night parliamentary sessions, which included long filibustering speeches from Opposition Members, scenes of grave disorder involving the entanglement of Deputy Speaker, Sir Gordon Touche, in procedural difficulties, all of which brought us no nearer whatsoever to the solution of the intractable problems of the National Health Service.

At last, as a residual beneficiary of this uproar, and consequent on the extension of the debate, I was able, on its second day, to make a speech about the Health Service. Apart from registering for the third time my opinion that the Guillebaud Report (which in 1957 had reported on the structure of the Service in thoroughly complacent fashion) was 'one of the most disastrous documents of modern times', my speech on this occasion was somewhat less interesting than the critical comments of Dr. J. Dickson Mabon, the youthful Labour Member for Greenock, in reply to what I said:

'May I say that the majority of my colleagues in the medical profession do not share the view of the hon. Member for Carlisle. The men in medicine to-day are not the same men that were there in 1948; they have changed a lot. A decade has passed; some have died, some have retired and others have taken their place. There is a new generation and an entirely different attitude to the National Health Service. Those who were not happy with it at the beginning have seen it in practice and now welcome it.'

Dr. Mabon (whose pre-parliamentary medical experience is conspicuous mainly by its absence in the reference books) spoke, apparently oblivious of the doctors' discontent, the expression of which at that time was confined to the correspondence columns of the *British Medical Journal*, but which eventually boiled over into the threat of mass withdrawal four years later. Remote from medical realities as he proved himself to be, he was, on the other hand, considerably more cogent when he told me that I was 'so dreadfully lost in the present political world'. Faced with the obscurantism of the Ministry of Health, I was becoming increasingly bewildered.

Undeterred, however, by the animadversions of Dr. Mabon, I continued to put my views on the position of the general practitioner in the full day's National Health Service debate, which occurred on 11th July 1961. Extracts from my speech are perhaps relevant in the light of subsequent events.

'We have heard in previous debates (I comment) of the alleged drop in status of the general practitioner. There is a large element of truth in that.

'What is a fact to-day is that the doctor's work is, under present conditions, dull, dreary and to a large extent disheartening. It consists, not in coping with the difficult and interesting problems in medicine which he has seen in hospitals and has been trained to deal with, but largely in dealing with certificates, repeat prescriptions, specialists' letters and pharmaceutical circulars.

'It is also beyond doubt that the work of the general practitioner is overweighted with minor maladies at the expense of what the doctor feels is his real work which is drifting into the hands of the hospitals. He has the feeling that his status and his work are being reduced to that of a medical orderly, while circumstances do not allow him under present conditions, particularly in general practices in the towns, to do the work for which he is trained.'*

I went on then to talk of the importance of retaining the smaller hospitals in the country districts as important centres where general practitioners can keep up their standards through having the continuing opportunity to do interesting work, of the development of diagnostic centres; of the disastrous situation whereby the stage in the patient's diagnosis of separation of major illness from minor illness has gone beyond the general practitioners and into the hospitals; and of the inefficiency and waste in money thereby involved.

Finally, I deplored the capitation fee and suggested that doctors might be paid fees for item of service for special work on top of the capitation fee**: I likewise deplored the opportunity missed by the Pilkington Committee on Doctors' and

* *Hansard*: Vol. 644, Column 298.
** This was eventually adopted in 1966.

Dentists' Pay in not sorting out the method of doctors' payment as well as the amount.

Such is only a brief *précis* of the twenty-five minute speech. A lifetime of experience, years of reading and special study, hours of previous preparation had gone into this speech. I regard it as the best and most authoritative contribution to debates which I made in my nine years in the House of Commons.

It would be wrong for me, even now, these several years later, to conceal the disappointment which I felt at its reception—or, at least, its absence of reception.

Called by Mr. Speaker at 7.30 p.m., I could not have had more than twelve to fifteen Members listening to me: the majority of my colleagues being by that time at dinner. The Parliamentary Secretary to the Ministry, the late Miss Edith Pitt, in replying to the debate, answered the majority of the points raised in speeches with her usual courtesy, but did not refer to any single point of mine. As for Press reports, there was a complete silence as to any single word I said in the whole of the national Press, with the exception of the customary inch in *The Times* and even here the report referred only to an unimportant side-comment about German doctors.

Though doctors were shouting their heads off in private, filling the correspondence columns of the medical papers with their complaints and unburdening themselves of their woes to whomsoever would listen to them, it was just not recognised in official circles there was any such thing as a discontented doctor! As far as I was concerned, I was left with the feeling that I had been talking to thin air. Instead of waiting for hours on a parliamentary bench for my turn to speak, I might just as well have been outside in the air—perhaps playing golf?

I found the opportunity to comment upon this situation in a letter to the *Sunday Telegraph* on 14th January 1962. Suitably entitled (by the paper) A VOICE IN THE WILDERNESS, this was the letter:

Sir, Mr. Peregrine Worsthorne's comments on the

frustrating nature of the pursuit of politics at the present time ('Your Government Calling', Jan. 7) are well timed.

Ministers are, as he suggests, the proper recipients of sympathy in their difficulties in getting themselves and their message across to the public. What, however, of the parliamentary backbencher?

It is not, after all, to be expected that, when one is called to speak at 7 or 8 p.m. with perhaps a dozen colleagues occupying the House and with merely a subsequent 'also spoke' in the national Press and perhaps a half-inch report in the medical papers, one's impact can be other than a minimal one in present circumstances. It is, in fact, the nearest thing to talking to oneself that can possibly be imagined.

As Mr. Worsthorne says, it is only our more puerile performances at Westminster that attract public attention. Thus, while serious comment goes unheeded, the spectacle in which the Labour Opposition scored the 'triumph' of discomforting the Deputy Speaker in last summer's debate on the National Health Insurance Contributions Bill made nation-wide headlines.

The only people who benefit from this state of affairs are the permanent bureaucracy.

'While Parliament wrangles, we administrators get on with the job of providing a Health Service', so shape the distinguished guest (possibly unaware there was a medical Member of Parliament present) to a dinner party of a well-known medical society, commenting on this event. He was not entirely wrong, but the slant given by the public 'image' of Parliament presented in the news columns enhanced his point of view.

DONALD McI. JOHNSON,
House of Commons, S.W.1.

My letter in the *Sunday Telegraph* must, however, be numbered amongst 'famous last words'.

There is little use in filling these pages with the detailed chronicle of my subsequent ill success. There was the occasion

when I found myself standing on my feet in the House, unnoticed, while the debate, which had nominally ten minutes
to go, was adjourned by Mr. Speaker* just the same: there
was the debate in which I was reprimanded by Mr. Speaker
in my endeavour to extend its somewhat narrow terms which
referred to medical research—but research on kidney disease
alone: the further debate when I found myself to be the only
potential speaker on the Government side of the House who
was left 'uncalled' at the end of the day.

Simultaneously, I was pursuing my campaign at Question
Time at which, thanks to its fixed rules and procedures, I
at least had my say. For instance, at a date as early as 26th
February 1957, I had asked the Prime Minister (Mr. Harold
Macmillan), 'whether the terms of reference of the Royal
Commission on Doctors' Remuneration would include an
examination of the method as well as the amount of re-
muneration'.**

On 24th November 1958, was my first Parliamentary
Question—the first Parliamentary Question ever, as far as I know
—to the Minister of Health on the subject of medical emigration.

Mr. Derek Walker-Smith, then Minister, 'had no reliable
evidence' on the subject. Mr. J. R. Tilney (Conservative M.P.
for the Wavertree Division of Liverpool) suggested to the
Minister in a supplementary question that emigration to the
Commonwealth countries should be encouraged by his
Department.

On 10th December 1962, I asked the Minister—by now
Mr. Enoch Powell—'if he is aware of the continued high rate
of emigration of British doctors and the problem of staffing
in the National Health Service thereby created and what
steps he is taking within the full context of a free society to
keep doctors in Great Britain'.

'No, sir', replied Mr. Enoch Powell, 'this does not arise.'***

Though what 'did not arise' is not quite clear. In reply
to my supplementary question to ask for more data, the

* The Speaker at that time was the late Sir Harry Hylton-Foster.
** *Hansard*: Vol. 565, Columns 1040, 1041.
*** *Hansard*: Vol. 669, Column 27.

Minister assured me that 'the number of students who take up residence abroad is quite small, about 6 per cent'.

Thus for my share in this long protracted battle. The iconoclast on this occasion was, however, not myself, but Dr. John Seale whom I was to meet for the first time, consequent on ITN interest in this problem, in an interview with John Whale on TV later that same week. Dr. John Seale, even more sceptical than I was of the Minister's figures, in the most 'disloyal' fashion decided to obtain information at the receiving end, consequent on which he wrote to the Registrars of the Medical Councils and other authorities throughout the Commonwealth and in the United States of America to ascertain the number of British-trained doctors who had registered yearly in their respective territories. His conclusions, published in a paper in the *British Medical Journal* in March 1962, were to the effect that 600 doctors born and trained in Great Britain and Ireland were emigrating annually, which was about five times the rate in the 1930s and about five times the current rate of general emigration.

'Its errors will be persisted in long after they have been revealed,' spoke 'Enoch the Evangelist' of the national plan, 'because governments are the slowest of all creatures to admit themselves mistaken and a state plan of all plans the most inflexible.'

'So much nonsense,' declared Mr. Enoch Powell—'Enoch the Minister'—ridiculing 'recent writings about emigration of doctors' in a speech to the Faculty of Anaesthetists four days after Dr. Seale had published his paper.

So the ding-dong struggle went on about the doctors who were preferring to emigrate rather than enter the British National Health Service, with Mr. Kenneth Robinson, later Minister of Health in the Labour Government, joining in to dismiss emigration figures which differed from the Ministry of Health's as 'superficial and misleading' in an article in *Medical Care* in 1963.

Since then, however, Mr. Robinson has had occasion to think, and to speak, differently on the subject of doctors' emigration.

It was only in 1966, some eight years after I had first

mentioned the matter in the House of Commons, that a final
arbiter with authoritative information appeared on the scene.
This was the Seventh Report of 'The Review on Doctors' and
Dentists' Remuneration' published in Mary 1966, in paragraph 57 of which are quoted the statistics of the Overseas
Migration Board for 1964, which show a net loss of 900 doctors
with United Kingdom passports, counterblanced only by a
net gain of 300 doctors with passports of other countries.
Total net loss, 600 doctors in 1964.

'We find it very disquieting', say the Review Body, 'that
the net outflow of doctors with United Kingdom passports
should be so high in relation to the output of qualified British
doctors from British medical schools.'

The arguments still continue in a minor key, but the situation
has been disquieting enough for the Government to have
offered doctors substantial rises in pay in 1966. Though
whether these alone will effect the cure of a now desperate
situation still remains to be seen.

Finally, I put it all down in a book. This was *The British
National Health Service: Friend or Frankenstein?* published in 1962.
I had during my years in Parliament, frequently had occasion
to call to mind the warning of the late Jonathan Cape, publisher
of my first book, that publishing and politics did not mix well.
But now my publishing facilities came to the rescue. For,
thanks to this book and the recognition which it received in
appropriate places, such as the review by Tom Lindsay on
the centre page of the *Daily Telegraph*, I was able to make
more impact than I might have done in one hundred years of
exclusively parliamentary endeavour. Though even this was
little enough. However, as a matter of incidental interest,
later in 1962, my book resulted in an invitation from that sturdy
body of citizens the 'Keep Our Doctors Association' to speak to
audiences in Saskatchewan at the time of the 'medicare'
crisis in that Province. Both here and in other parts of Canada
I visited, I still found that the glad message was assiduously
being given out by the British Information Services that the
doctors in Great Britain were entirely satisfied with their lot
under the National Health Service!

I often think what I had to say in Canada at a crucial moment in the development of that country's medical affairs had more impact and more bearing on the future than any words of mine to the closed minds of those who were in charge of affairs at home.* For I have to report that, much as I am in accord with Enoch the Evangelist, with Enoch the Minister it was a different state of affairs. The following passage from Hansard of 11th March 1963 is perhaps typical:

Dr. Johnson asked the Minister of Health if he will abolish the prescription charge in respect of a specified list of essential drugs.

Mr. Powell: No, sir.

Dr. Johnson: Will my right honourable Friend look into this matter at greater length than is indicated by his reply?

Mr. Powell: The brevity of my reply is no measure of the length of consideration given to the Question.**

('Will my right Hon. Friend accept my congratulations for the brevity and effectiveness of his answers?' intervened Sir James Duncan, Conservative M.P. for South Angus, later in this series of Questions. But had I, in the meantime, heard the microphones of the Chamber echoing those old-fashioned words, 'The Gentlemen in Whitehall Know Best'?)

*　*　*　*　*

To sum up, my book and my other efforts got me as far abroad as Saskatchewan and the Pacific Coast of Canada. They obtained for me at that same time the accolade of being 'elected' as 'straw' Minister of Health in the poll of the readers of Edward Martell's *The New Daily* that was held in that paper in early 1963 for the most fitting occupants of ministerial posts—ahead of the Minister himself (Mr. Enoch Powell) by 'a considerable number of votes'. But, in Parliament itself, they did not get me beyond sitting silent and uncalled on the back benches during debates and listening to the

* I much appreciated my inclusion amongst the 'Acknowledgments' in the Report of the Canadian Royal Commission on the Health Services under the Chairmanship of Judge Emmett Hall.

** *Hansard*: Vol. 673, Column 949.

monosyllabic replies of Mr. Enoch Powell at Question Time.

'I doubt whether this will have much influence with Mr. Macmillan,' was my comment on the result of *The New Daily* poll. And, of course, it did not. It was, alas, to prove something of a crown of thorns.

Should a doctor be Minister of Health? The very suggestion has been 'scouted' as an offence to our traditional 'amateur system of Government'. Though what this latter is, other than a part of the archaic web in which our country has become enmeshed, it is difficult to say. Personally, I cannot see that Parliament can effectively control a Health Service in any other way than by the appointment of a doctor as Minister of Health: for, with any other type of appointment, the power inevitably passes elsewhere to the Minister's medical 'advisers' —and, after all, look what a mess *they* are making!

This, however, must be regarded as a side issue.

The issue that did arise in my case was whether, under circumstances in which Parliament was nominally sponsoring a National Health Service, a qualified and experienced doctor could find any scope at all for constructive work as a Member of Parliament. The answer to this was plain and clear: there was in the 1959–64 Parliament no way whatsoever in which this could be done.

Lest I be thought to be grinding solely an individual axe, I refer to the Question which I asked Mr. Robin Turton, then Minister of Health, on 4th June 1957: that he would give the names of the members of the eleven working parties and committees which were then due to report on different aspects of the National Health Service. These 125 names, which I have published as a special appendix to *A Doctor in Parliament*, include naturally many distinguished medical men and women, but amongst them there is no single medical Member of Parliament. Indeed, there are only two Members of Parliament in all, both of whom, it scarcely need be said, were Socialists —this after some six years of Conservative Government.

I revert to the thesis of Professor Philip Buck of Stanford University in his book to which I have referred in Chapter Six. His conclusion was that British parliamentarians were insufficiently professional. Was I an amateur or was I a professional? Did I eventually have to go because I was too amateur as a politician; or because I was too professional as a doctor? Probably I was too amateur for the professionals and too professional for the amateurs. I was a nuisance to any lay Minister through what I knew. But I was more than that. I was a standing offence to the system inasmuch as I cut across the old English system of Gentlemen and Players. In its manifestation as a political system, on one side are the Gentlemen—the Members of Parliament: on the other side are the Players—the civil servants. But for a Gent to step out of line and insist that he was a Player, or for a Player to pretend to be a Gentlemen were of course equally obnoxious. As a doctor in Parliament, asking awkward questions, I was doing both these.

But whether I was a Gentleman or a Player, my personal position was an increasingly invidious one. What can be more irksome than persistent frustration? To be in the position of having on the one hand the honourable position of a Member of the Parliament, yet finding that this honour was devoid of content in all practical matters, so that not only was I conspicuously ignored in the political field, but also, in the circumstances of the National Health Service and the widespread power of the central administration, in professional life also, was intolerable.

A doctor in Parliament had, so it seemed, one of three choices. He could abandon his political interest in Health altogether and take up alternative parliamentary pursuits, in the manner that several of my medical political colleagues had done with considerable success: or he could merely 'belt up' in his criticisms and become subservient to the totalitarian health administration, fundamentally as he might disagree with it: or he could give up the political struggle and resign from Parliament.

'Don't resign. Wait until they throw you out,' declared the late David Kirkwood, formerly of Clydeside fame.

It need scarcely be said—but I am bound to say it in the light of the accusations levelled at me by ignorant people at a later date—that this quandary, in which none of the alternatives was acceptable to me, involved many pilgrimages to the office of the Chief Whip to discuss the situation.

But whether it was the 'abrasive' Ted Heath, or his successor, the more genial Martin Redmayne, there seemed no answer. Different Chief Whips have had different methods of lining up the disgruntled and the discontented in their flock. Martin Redmayne's principal weapon was that of charm: and it was he of whom I saw most, inasmuch as it was he who occupied this difficult position during the 1959–64 Parliament, when my own problems became acute. No thunderbolts greeted one as one came to talk with Martin Redmayne. On the contrary, five minutes conversation in his sanctum would induce an irresistible relaxation of tension, while after ten minutes one would find oneself believing that all was for the best in the best of all possible worlds—that, at least, was the effect which he had on me. This state of euphoria would persist until some half-hour later when, once again back in the bleak lobbies of the House, one would 'come to', only to realise that the customary problems were still there, in as insoluble form as ever.

It was with unfailing good-temper that Martin Redmayne bore with me in the face of what could only have seemed to him conspicuous obstinacy. While I on the other hand made no headway against this unfailing *sang froid*.

I waited and waited in a state of almost suspended animation throughout the years of this tiresome Parliament for someone to throw me out.

I was not, however, to wait indefinitely.

CHAPTER EIGHT

WELCOME TO HARMONY

IN OLDEN days, as we know, the recalcitrant 'politico' up against authoritarian rule quickly found himself cooling his heels in the Tower of London. At a later date Parliament's own sanction of its privileges was enforced with the aid of a dungeon beneath Big Ben for the reception of those who failed to respect its dignity. Only a little way further westwards again are the underground passages of the Interview Rooms of the House of Commons, a very special place of purgatory suspended between the sacred precincts of the House and the outside world, whither tend to be driven those suffering under the more subtle persecution of a modern bureaucracy.

It was in this haven of comparative peace, two storeys below the Principal Floor of the House, where one might talk in a reasonably normal tone of voice, without anyone saying 'Sh-sh' on account of the danger of being overheard, where one could read and write with only a modicum of interruption such as the heavy tramp of feet up and down the central aisle in the Members' Library, and whither no member of the Whips' Office was ever seen to penetrate, that I found a place of withdrawal during my final years in Parliament.

Here, I was one of a small, but select band. For, during these years, the Interview Rooms' passages housed an interesting company of Members of like habits, but varying political faiths—students, writers and thinkers of both political poles who found themselves in each other's company. To the right was Henry Kerby in the famous Room 12, which will surely deserve a special plaque at some future date, John

Biggs-Davison* two or three rooms away and, adjacent to him, Ronald Russell**; while strung along the passage was the left-wing, Barbara Castle, Fenner Brockway and occasionally other characters of the same faith. For the majority of the day, in this strangely assorted company, the lion lay down with the lamb in happy contentment and no political differences disturbed the atmosphere of personal harmony that prevailed throughout.

It was only late in the evening when, after 7 p.m. the company started to dwindle and depart their several ways, that I would find myself alone, either waiting for a vote to take place, or merely waiting for Bill Williams,*** my 'pair', to send me the signal that he was ready to depart home to our common destination, Sutton. A lifetime of evening attendance at trade union meetings had made Bill Williams reluctant to tear himself away from the talkative male companionship that he so much enjoyed and, even when there was no vote, he was a dilatory leaver from the House to catch the 9.18 p.m. at Victoria. On those rare occasions when we caught the 7.18—the only other evening train on which we could use our first-class tickets—it was a gala evening indeed.

It was at such times that I started to ponder. I consoled myself that I had found the best place in the House of Commons —away from it all. It was, as I have already indicated, the only place to find true peace and quiet for writing letters, sorting papers, reading the proofs of my firm's books. On the other hand it gradually sank in on me that these proofs, these letters, these papers could be read, written, sorted in greater comfort and in the even better company of my dear wife at home. Was this *really* the only place to be? Or was I, in effect, incarcerated in a political prison, endowed with an honorable but empty label which merely camouflaged the fact that I was undergoing preventive detention by the ties of the Party Whip.

* John Biggs-Davison, Conservative M.P. for Chigwell Division of Essex. A courageous resister of Mr. Macmillan's African policy.
** Sir Ronald Russell, Conservative M.P. for Wembley (South), Joint Secretary of the 1922 Committee.
*** The late W. R. Williams, Labour M.P. for Openshaw Division of Manchester.

Inevitably likewise, it occurred to me that, at a time when every Government statement, and indeed every Opposition statement, clamoured for maximum use of manpower and glorified opportunity, the Government itself set a somewhat bizarre example in the way that it stultified the manpower immediately available to it. Certainly, there was no need for anyone with medical degrees and legal qualifications or professional experience of any kind, to fulfil the demands of this sort of occupation.

I try not to exaggerate. However, not only was I personally detained, but all orthodox channels for self-expression were likewise barred to me. Platforms throughout the country were fenced in by the Party machine, appointments in connection with the Health Service were blocked by the veto of a bureaucracy resentful of my criticisms, debates in Parliament were negatived by the unhappy chance of my claims to speak not being acknowledged by Speaker Hylton-Foster.

I owe much to those who provided me with an escape mechanism from this restricted situation. There was the hospitality of the correspondence columns of the *Daily Telegraph* which, under the editorship of Sir Colin Coote, were opened to expressions of discontent in Conservative circles which could find no outlet elsewhere, thus providing a safety valve of unparallelled worth, not only to the complainers, but to the Party itself, sliding rapidly, as it was, into Party totalitarianism. There was the Society for Individual Freedom with its energetic secretary, Lilian Hardern, who joined forces with me in our campaign for the appointment of an Ombudsman, in connection with which on 19th May 1961,* I sponsored the first debate in the House of Commons on this important reform which is now realised. Finally, as I shall have to tell later, there were the platforms provided by Edward Martell in his National Fellowship.

Once again, also, my publishing business came to the rescue. Indeed, I do not know what I should have done without it. For what else was there to do in filling in the weary time spent in the Interview Rooms' passages than to write yet another

* *Hansard*: Vol. 640, Columns 1693–1756.

book: it was a comforting thought to know that such a book would at least be published.

I can now, at this distance of time, come quite clean that it was I who did write that book, whose mysterious author the representative of the Charles Greville Diary of the *Daily Mail* took some three days in tracing down to make his story 'Dr. Johnson, M.P., and the Secret of a Satirical Tale of Harmony' the principal item of this column on Monday, 3rd December 1962.

But, apart from this welcome but tardy effort, which appeared two months after publication, *Welcome to Harmony* had been no 'rave' in the Press at all. Maybe the publication of a book by stealth is hardly the most successful way to promote it: maybe the Press was obsessed by fear of 'privilege' at that time, but the fact is that *Welcome to Harmony* (in my own fond imagination another *Gulliver's Travels* or an *Animal Farm*, lost thus far to literature) was only read by a few hundred people. It is accordingly permissible for me to reproduce its theme.

Welcome to Harmony is the story of Harmony Hall, its Headmaster (illustrated by Michael ffolkes as a bearded figure with a close resemblance to Mr. Harold Macmillan), its Second Master, Mr. Bowers, and its principal Games Master, Mr. Hampstead, on the one hand: its pupils on the other. Amongst the pupils is Ewart Greenhalgh, hailing from a chemist's shop in a North of England town, isolated amongst his school-fellows with their more splendid backgrounds, a stranger to their ways and uninitiated into their customs. 'The Head' is fond of speechifying, whether in public or in private and his subject is 'Harmony': 'The Head' on 'Harmony' entrances the boys and hypnotises the parents. Indeed the parents are so hypnotised that they are oblivious to the fact that their boys are learning nothing at all, inasmuch as they spend their time attending the 'Harmony Classes' at which they are merely taught to make paper chains and do basket work. The whole school attend the Harmony Classes with the exception of those who, somehow or other, attain to Mr. Bowers' form at the top of the school: these selected few are the only ones who have the benefit of a proper education.

There is a secondary plot about 'the pots'—the silver cups that are the reward of victory in the regular games that take place between Harmony Hall and their rival and less pretentious establishment 'Loggerheads Lodge'. There is the theft of the 'pots' and the distress that this occasions.

The main story, however, concerns the adventures of Ewart Greenhalgh, his chagrin at not being allowed to learn, his aspirations to Mr. Bowers' form and his final distressing realisation that, for reasons which he could not himself understand, he could never consider himself amongst the select. There is his pathetic subterfuge in reading textbooks (forbidden literature for the main part of the school) disguised as books of entertainment: and his final unmasking by Mr. Hampstead while he was reading that famous Macmillan publication, Hall and Knight's *Algebra*, disguised as R. L. Stevenson's *Treasure Island*. The *dénouement* comes when Ewart, chased by a horde of boys and masters yelling 'Oick' and 'Sweatgut', tumbles into the muddy waters of the lake on the far side of the playing field. Does he get out of the lake? That is left for the reader to speculate.

It was a satire on the House of Commons at that time, but it had a further background of an alarmingly real character. For instance, this school that was the House of Commons was also my preparatory school, the Cheltenham Junior School, during the time of the First World War between 1913 and 1917, the years of my own residence at that institution. As the story worked itself out as I wrote, the resemblance between the scenes based on incidents that had actually happened at school and other scenes based on other incidents at the House of Commons was not only close, it was positively alarming. It might be the House of Commons which I was satirising, 'The Head' might be more like Harold Macmillan than he was like the head of my own school (though he was not so unlike to the latter as all that), but the whole story worked itself out against the passages, the dining hall and the 'sweatrooms' of the Cheltenham Junior School in a quite fantastic way.

There was, for instance, the Italian boy who pinched the bottom of one of the maids and who was isolated in disgrace from the rest of the school because of his tendency to mix with the 'scivs'—I hasten to say that this was both written and published well over a year before the Profumo scandal was heard of. But there we are!

And there, streaking across the playing field with the yelling crowd after him, who was that? That was I. An 'oick' then—a person of no background or social connections—and an 'oick' now; a 'sweatgut' then—one who liked to work and learn—and a 'sweatgut' now—working in isolation instead of indulging in the various gregarious activities in which it was open for me to participate. This was not only a parody of the House of Commons as I knew it; it was also a parody of my own career and my own strivings. While the final tumble into the pond midst shouts of derision—who will, after reading my story, deny that that, at least, was prophetic?

There were other parallels in *Welcome to Harmony*: there was Ewart's father, the naïve Mr. Greenhalgh, the provincial town chemist and doting parent who lived in a world of fond illusion as far as Harmony Hall was concerned and who could not be brought to the realisation that his son was unhappy and stultified at the grand establishment to which he had laboured so hard to send him. Ewart's father was my own father, a doctor in Bury, Lancashire, of so long ago, with his similar delusions about the Junior School at Cheltenham; he was also a parody of those curiously fond people of the Carlisle Conservative Association, who had struggled so hard to elect me to my present eminence, who cherished me so warmly on my visits to them in Carlisle, yet who were almost totally disinterested in any part of my experiences in Parliament that conflicted with the scheme of things in their own imaginings.

As they will be looming larger and larger into this story, it is well that we should endeavour to understand the point of view of these devoted, but narrow and naïve people. To the 'with it' people of to-day, doubtless James Branch Cabell's *Jurgen* is 'old hat'—pallid stuff, maybe, in comparison with the effusions of the band-wagon writers of the sexual revolution.

In the early 1920s, however, *Jurgen* with its ironic humour was one of the ice-breakers of the deep freeze of the Puritan heritage: and the grandmother of James Branch Cabell's hero sat in her citadel, surrounded by walls within which everything existed according to her own imaginings, regardless of the realities outside and beyond.

In the same manner, politically speaking, the world of the members of my Carlisle Conservative Association was the world of Jurgen's grandmother. On my visits to Carlisle, when the subject of Westminster came up, they would talk to me just in the same way as my father would talk to me about Cheltenham College on my return home from school. In this world of their own imaginings, Westminster was a place of blessedness in which their Member lived in utmost bliss, attending jamborees in evening dress, hob-nobbing with prominent socialites, shaking hands with titled people—a place, in fact, which corresponded with their own idea of Heaven.

If one did not fit in with this conception of a Conservative paradise, one ceased somehow to exist and became eliminated in their minds as a real person. I can well remember how, during one of my earlier years in Carlisle, when Betty and I attended the Conservative Association annual dance, our statement that this was the first occasion on which we had worn evening dress for nine months or more was greeted with dismay and incredulity. It was from that moment, I truly believe, that my reputation started to slide.

But, of course, Parliament at Westminster, whatever it is like, is not like that at all—not for the boy from the Provinces, anyway. But one could not say so, any more than, during the whole of my seven years at Cheltenham College between 1913 and 1920, I could return to Lancashire and tell my father of the realities of a public school of that time. Indeed, one of my worst moments in Carlisle—and this still in my 'honeymoon' period—was when I endeavoured in the most discreet fashion imaginable and in a full spirit of helpfulness, to inform my lady supporters at their annual general meeting about Parliament and parliamentary procedures. Even this harmless exercise was the occasion of acidulous comments from my lady chairman; I was at the time completely mystified at the extent of the bitterness evoked from so inoffensive a dissertation.

This first *contretemps*, as I have said, occurred during my early days in Parliament. It can be well understood that, as I became more outspoken, as my novelty waned, so in certain sections of my Association did my popularity slip. For, given the premises I have just set out, it will be understandable that the least hint of criticism or discontent tended to be regarded as ingratitude of a monstrous character. Honeymoon conditions between my Carlisle supporters and myself would clearly only exist as long as I could act my part in the charade.

Unfortunately this was not possible indefinitely. In the aura of excitement and public sympathy which had accompanied my mental health campaigning during my first term in Parliament, I had managed the situation with some success. Aided by the prestige which I accumulated over this, I even induced my then friends on the Carlisle Conservative Executive Committee to pass a resolution—a very *strictly* private resolution, of course—indicating that they would like to see their M.P., in the light of his special knowledge and experience, have the opportunity to take a more vital part in health affairs and to send this to Lord Hailsham, Chairman of the Party. However, Lord Hailsham in his reply, a thoroughly unhelpful reply as I remember it, indicated that he was entirely mystified as to what they were talking about and there the matter dropped. 'Dr. Johnson attends the Party Health Committee,' said Lord Hailsham, as if that was the ultimate answer: that was so, but I had been warned at an early stage in my parliamentary life that I should not misunderstand the purpose of the Party Health Committee—its main purpose was, needless to say, 'to support the Minister'. Over nine years I never knew at any time any Minister to be influenced by anything said on this Committee.

However, the question could not, on my side, be dropped as easily as that. Following the 1959 Election and my re-election for a further term in Parliament, as I saw it, the position had to be faced. At a private dinner party for my principal supporters, I took the opportunity to make it clear to them that, though the Conservative Party might, as it claims, be the Party of Opportunity, it was not proving to be the Party of Opportunity for me. I added that I could not, in these circumstances, promise to continue to represent them in further Parliaments unless there was some change in this situation.

I was to receive no bouquets for my candour: and we shall hear more of this dinner party later on. Looking back, I suppose that I could have done almost anything but what I actually did. Had I had a personal scandal to confess, a divorce or anything of that kind, these people would have 'understood' and stood by me. But to cast doubt on 'The Party', that was another matter. I had broken the code: in rejecting the illusion of beatitude to which I was expected to subscribe, I was undermining the legend on which their faith was founded. I was now a person to be watched—and watched carefully. In the meantime, no breath of this discontent could be allowed to leak out; supporters must not be alienated; the Party workers must not be upset. By direct and friendly persuasion, or even by implied threats, my tongue must be stilled by these people so fearful of the truth. I was already the rebel archangel, poised like Lucifer before his Fall.

Only one thing saved me from an immediate challenge: namely that nobody present in my audience on this occasion really believed that I meant what I said. That I would abandon the state of bliss which was considered to be my lot for reasons of a non-material and insubstantial nature was something that was not within the range of experience of any of those present. I was clearly (in their minds) bluffing, even though bluffing dangerously. I would undoubtedly 'come round' (so they must have thought) if firmly dealt with, as many a recalcitrant party politician, when faced with the might of the Party machine, has so often 'come round' before.

None the less, from then on I was a marked man. As this 1959–64 Parliament progressed, I was conscious of the net that was closing in on me. I had entered a declining spiral from which there was no escape. How much my private

warning to the Officers of my Association filtered through to
Party Headquarters in London, I do not know. I suspect a
good bit. For gradually, the same sort of thing started to
happen to me in Carlisle, as I have already complained
happened to me in the House of Commons. The distinguished
Party speakers who had thronged my platform during my
early days in Carlisle ceased to appear. Such enthusiasm as
there had been for my success in the field of mental health
legislation waned perceptibly. The diffidence in asking me to
speak on Party platforms intensified to the extent that I was
finally left with only one platform a year, the Annual General
Meeting of the Carlisle Conservative Association, at which I
could not very well be dispensed with. If I had anything to say,
I must speak then, or for ever hold my peace—until the
following year.

My visits to Carlisle became more and more abbreviated to
a Saturday morning spent interviewing constituents with their
grievances (ironically enough, I was expected to listen and
attend to everyone else's grievances, but not to have any
grievances of my own); to a Saturday afternoon spent dis-
cussing the situation with my friend and agent, Stanley
Walker;* and to a Saturday evening visiting the Denton Holme
Conservative Working Men's Club on a strictly social basis
prior to catching my train home at midnight. During my first
year or two in Parliament the Denton Holme Club had always
insisted on a political speech at the week-end, but not now.
There was no question of animosity against me here; it was
merely that I must not interrupt the bingo.

This became the pattern in my relationship with my
constituency over a number of years. It was one in which I
acquiesced, inasmuch as I could do the chores of my distant
constituency in a minimum of time, so that, at least, I could
get back home on Sunday morning and have one day at the
week-end in which I could see something of my own family.
But even such a programme was arduous enough when, as
often as not, following a week of late nights, I would find
myself on Friday evening walking up and down Platform 13 at
Euston Station between 11.30 p.m. and midnight at all times

* S. B. Walker unfortunately was to leave Carlisle before 1963.

of the year and in all weathers, waiting for the 12.10 a.m. sleeper train to enter the station.

What I have described is the normal path for the rebel M.P.—down the slippery slope, then the long drop into the still waters of the canal of oblivion at the end.

However, I was by no means the only person in the Conservative Party who found themselves thwarted during those years and helpless against a political machine which, propelled towards its own destruction by Mr. Harold Macmillan, had set itself to ignore all warnings. Not every Conservative supporter found himself able to subscribe readily to 'The Wind of Change', 'the-never-had-it-so-goodism' of giving way to unrealistic trade union claims and the wholesale uncritical adoption of the welfare state—such as had happened, for instance, with the National Health Service.

Into the vacuum of political leadership thus created there had stepped the dynamic personality of Edward Martell, an exotic figure to the world of parliamentary politics, yet one who, by his reputation as an organiser and a man of action, combined with a considerable measure of political ability, formed a rallying point for the anti-Macmillan discontent.

It would take a separate book to recount the full story of the projects that emanated from the restless brain of Edward Martell, who, at the time of which I now speak, had reached the peak of his influence as a redeemer of the Conservative Party. But, eventually, on 1st January 1962 his kaleidoscopic series of movements and organisations became coalesced into the National Fellowship, a campaigning force dedicated to the revival of the Conservative Party on traditional lines. The National Fellowship came on to the scene at a time of maximum discordance in the Conservative Party over the policies of Mr. Harold Macmillan in general, and that of Mr. Iain Macleod (then Secretary of State for the Colonies) in Africa in particular. I still have amongst my political trophies (side by side with the yellow lapel badge of the Carlisle Conservative Association) the fetchingly designed badge of this movement with its inscribed motto of 'RESURGAT BRITANNIA'.

The National Fellowship drew both financial and personal

support from thousands of Conservatives of position and substance throughout the country: and this included the sympathy of many in influential places in the Conservative Party itself. It was, however, Edward Martell's misfortune that no one with a positive political stake in the Party would commit themselves to open support. The National Fellowship had a distinguished list of open supporters, yet the list, which was published in full with its numerous titled folk and people of elevated military and naval rank, had scarcely a person with any political know-how. Its money chests were at that time bulging and there was widespread apprehension that the contributions paid to it were detracting from the income of the Conservative Party itself: yet, when it came to definitive political action to make use of these funds, such as putting up an independent candidate at a by-election, or even a number of candidates at the General Election, there were strong inhibitions—occasioned by the initial certainty that these subscriptions would vanish over-night if such action caused a split in the Conservative vote and the loss of a seat to the Labour Party.

Personally I had no inhibitions about supporting the National Fellowship. As I have already said, it gave me an outlet. The meetings which Edward could gather at the Caxton Hall more or less at the drop of a hat, and at which Henry Kerby and I were the principal speakers, were meetings of a size that any Cabinet Minister would have been flattered to speak to. The only minor snag was that, in contrast to C.N.D. gatherings of perhaps one-quarter the size, no National Press report was vouchsafed to them. They were, however, a lively change from sitting forlornly in the Interview Rooms' passages.

I had nothing to lose but my chains. But, apart from the official disapproval, which was virtually guaranteed, it was, of course, considered dreadfully Right-Wing to be with the National Fellowship. This was perhaps natural on account of the type of support that it attracted. But the policies of the National Fellowship were proved not so much to be Right as, in the outcome, *right*—they were, in fact, merely common sense with a sprinkling of Edward Martell's old-fashioned Liberalism. I will take two examples.

As recently as 1962, for instance, it was considered to be the extreme of Right-Wingism to criticise the trade unions even for their most irresponsible actions. I had, I suppose, qualified for this label over the years in seconding the motion which Henry Kerby in his forthright fashion had put upon the Order Paper of the House of Commons.

This was the text of the Motion:

> ACTIVITIES OF TRADE UNIONS—That this House, having regard to the original conception of the trade unions as bodies with the proper purpose of providing negotiating machinery between employers and employees, but recognising that their organisation is now used by a handful of irresponsible persons in such a manner as can paralyse any section of industry, however vital to the national economy, urges Her Majesty's Government to recommend the setting up of a Royal Commission forthwith to inquire into the law relating to the legitimate activities of trade unions, with a view to preventing these being abused by unofficial strikes demarcation disputes and picketing and other customs leading to intimidation and victimisation of workers.

Year by year, when Parliament opened in the autumn this was Motion Number 1 on the Order Paper. This gave it no more chance of being debated than if it had been Motion Number 164, but it naturally brought it to special attention. Pretty well everyone on the Conservative side of the House agreed with the Motion, but it never collected more than half a dozen other signatures. Presumably the Whips made it clear that it was embarrassing to the Minister of Labour— indeed, before long, it was made directly clear to us that it WAS embarrassing to the Minister of Labour.

This was in 1959 by the newly appointed Minister of Labour, Mr. Edward Heath, himself. Henry and I, together with our co-signatory, Bill Yates,* were asked to attend an

---

* William Yates, Conservative M.P. for Wrekin Division of Shropshire, 1955–66.

interview at which it was suggested to us that we might withdraw our Motion. The Minister, a determined man, wrestled
mightily in argument with the unlikely trio whom he had
assembled. But on this occasion he wrestled in vain. The
Motion continued to appear.

It is ironical that it was left to a Labour Government to
implement this Motion by the announcement of Mr. Harold
Wilson on 2nd February 1965 of the appointment of a Royal
Commission under the Chairmanship of Lord Justice Donovan,
which is still waiting to report.

It was the same with Africa. The decolonisation policy of
the British Government in Africa was based, just as were many
of its welfare state policies at home, on outdated assumptions.
In this case, it was the assumption of the continuance in
perpetuity of the *pax Britannica* of the nineteenth century and
of the days when it was possible without difficulty to keep
Russia on her own side of the Dardanelles. This assumption,
of course, together with the positive fact of British hegemony
in Africa and the Middle East, on which it was based, went out
of the window at the time of 'Suez' in 1956. 'The Wind of
Change,' so assiduously fanned by the vanity of Mr. Harold
Macmillan, could only ensure, first that the African nations
reached the state of self-government while still in an immature
state of development, and second that there was a vacuum of
power in Africa which formed an irresistible temptation to the
promoters of power-hungry ideologies which had not yet been
heard of in the early days of this century.

I was no expert on Africa, but these arguments—so little
regarded by those who either out of devious intention, or from
youthful immaturity, were set on giving the Conservative
Party a progressive image—seemed to me obvious. While,
therefore, not venturing to place myself amongst the pundits,
I did everything within the limits of my position to help delay,
or even to stay, this baleful process while it was possible to do
so. Accordingly, Africa became one of my 'causes'—to sign my
name where I felt that it could be of use, to help occasionally
to tie up loose ends with an intervention, even to ask an
occasional Parliamentary Question.

The fact that this attitude automatically labelled me as 'Suez-minded', as the saying was, contributed substantially to my ultimate political doom.

But what had they got to say about all this in Carlisle? There is no doubt that the Officers of the Carlisle Conservative Association personally and severally agreed with me in such sentiments. But when, collectively, it came to consider my membership of the National Fellowship, then they did not agree—definitely not! However much I argued that the National Fellowship could scarcely be proscribed as long as it stuck to its declared intention of influencing opinion in the Party, it made no difference. It was, as I attempted to represent to them, merely a parallel movement to the Bow Group—an independent movement within the Conservative Party. But that argument cut remarkably little ice. It was carefully explained to me in one local official quarter that, of course, the Bow Group had Central Office approval, while the National Fellowship did not. This presumably was Conservative democracy. It was paradoxical, of course—a little uncanny indeed—that a movement along traditional Conservative lines should be frowned on when one which departed from these was so much *de rigueur*. But such was the peculiarity of the Conservative Party under Macmillan leadership.

On top of the more general apprehensions of the Carlisle Officers about the National Fellowship, they had a special apprehension of their own. My membership of the National Fellowship meant, apart from anything else, that here was I breaking loose from the gags and the chains that had hitherto bound me so successfully. I was speaking at mass meetings in London and you did not know where this sort of thing would stop! (As an incidental point, when Edward Martell was reported as saying that, as a sanction, members of the National Fellowship should withhold their subscriptions from Conservative Associations, the attitude of the Association Treasurer can have been nothing short of one of alarm.)

To be fair to them, it was not long before their apprehensions became clothed in substance. I have never been one for purely ineffective protests. It seemed to me that, as the fate of 'The Wind of Change' policy still hung in the balance, with as many objectors to it as there were supporters of it in the Conservative Party throughout the country, this was the time for a showdown. The following is a contemporary account from the *Carlisle Journal* of the annual general meeting of the Carlisle Conservative Association of 16th February 1962, some seven weeks after the foundation of the National Fellowship:

'As a rule Conservative Annual meetings are placid, cosy and a little dull. Half-way through the annual meeting of the Carlisle Conservatives last Friday, the Conservative M.P., Dr. Donald Johnson managed to make it anything but placid, cosy or dull.

'Stumbling over his words he told Carlisle's top Tories that in his opinion Conservatism was at the crossroads, and he wasn't at all sure whether he could go on being a Tory M.P.

'What he was going to do, he said, was to go on a "pilgrimage" for six to eight weeks. He would press questions to find out just where the Conservative Government stood on quite a few vital issues.

'Then he is going to come back and report to his Conservative supporters.

'The next item on the agenda said "Vote of thanks". Mr. H. W. Mawson, the chairman, got slowly to his feet. After what Dr. Johnson had just said, the conventional vote of thanks was out of the question.

'Mr. Mawson didn't even try:

' "I have heard what he has said and I can tell you that no such intimation of any such intention was made until the early part of this evening. I think this is unfortunate, but I respect the feelings of our M.P.", he said.

' "But it must not be taken at this stage that his views are the views of the Association. Very much consideration will have to be given by the Executive Committee to this question.

'What Dr. Johnson has said was, did he feel enthusiastic

enough to carry on and lead Carlisle Conservatives in the next election?

' "It can only be won by enthusiasm and I must assess myself in the light of this.

' "I think the Conservative Party is at the crossroads. When it took over ten years ago, it amended the most outrageous features of its Socialist heritage, but since then it has only been holding a watching brief.

' "It now has two choices—two clear choices.

' "It can swallow the Socialist State and dissolve British responsibility in Africa.

' "On the other hand, it can restore a property-owning democracy with its proper pride and, at the same time, take a more liberal view of the Health Service, with a more local control and greater medical freedom." '

Carlisle Journal, 23rd February 1962

I owe it to a further report to confirm that I included in the alternative policies 'the assurance that the multiracial Federation of the Rhodesias remains firmly in the hands of those who adhere to British ideals of good Government'.

So that was it! I had, at last, taken action—such action as was possible to me anyway.

If I stumbled over my words at this meeting, that was perhaps understandable. The hour immediately before the meeting, between the time when I had told the Officers of the Carlisle Association of my intention to make this statement— indeed, I had already sent a copy of my speech to the Press— and the opening of the meeting, was the most uncomfortable one which I have spent during the whole course of my political lifetime.

Bitter words were hurled at me about the embarrassment in which I had placed 'the Association': not to mention the Party as a whole.

However, they had no occasion to worry. For my 'pilgrimage' was a lonely one. Though the story of it was fully reported in the local Press and widely beyond that, I received no reaction to it whatsoever, apart from a few snide comments from my colleagues in the House of Commons.

I received no letter from any of my constituents, save only one from my good friend, Miss B——, who, though lively enough, was well beyond her seventieth year.

I was to report back to the Officers of my Association in two months' time and, as I started to circulate round Carlisle to meet the people, I found that the reaction to what I had said was not in any way hostile: indeed it was not a positive reaction at all. The simple assumption amongst my constituents was that I was already leaving them and, one after the other, they would approach me in the friendliest fashion and wish me well in my retirement.

As for my 'pilgrimage' and all that! It is said that the British Empire was acquired in a fit of absence of mind: this may or may not be true, but it was certainly lost that way. As I stood talking to my local friends in Carlisle, it was as if I were surrounded by political somnambulists. Africa and its problems were not mentioned.

I still think that my pilgrimage idea was a good one. It had endless possibilities that might have been developed. But not under these conditions! It was not long before I came to the conclusion that, since there was still half the length of a Parliament to go, there would be better occasions than the present one to pursue dissident action.

Thus, when one evening the phone rang and I received an invitation to 'a fireside chat' from my constituency Chairman, I accepted. 'A cosy and friendly fireside chat' I think he called it. But I had scarcely been seated near the flickering gas fire in the bleak upstairs room of the Conservative Office in Carlisle than I appreciated that this meeting was, intentionally or otherwise, merely a continuation of my uncomfortable conversation with them prior to the meeting on 16th February.

However, after a certain amount of indecisive bickering in regard to the liberty of speech of M.P.s, they issued the following statement adopting me as candidate for the subsequent Election:

'The members feel that Dr. Johnson has been a most

conscientious and hard-working and effective Member of Parliament for the City during his seven years of office and that he has on all important matters been a loyal supporter of the Government.'

But they would not have the National Fellowship! There was a special rider to that effect.

Indeed, it was fairly clear that, amongst the members mentioned, there were those who had much the same reservations about the situation on their side as I had on my own, as, once again, with nothing whatsoever achieved, I returned to sit, evening by evening, at my table-bench in the underground Interview Rooms' passage of the House of Commons.

CHAPTER NINE

THE DAY I MET MR. GINO MESSINA

AT THIS stage, more than half-way through my book, I have to emphasise what some may consider to be the old-fashioned trend of my ideas by weaving a further thread into my story in the most Dickensian fashion.

But why bring the Messinas into this story? They have nothing to do with the Conservative Party. Or Parliament, or the state of Government.

This was precisely the attitude of the Officers of the Carlisle Conservative Association when the headlines, two inches high, broke in the now defunct *Empire News* of Sunday, 3rd May 1959.

Oh, those headlines! This had been a most carefully edited piece of news in which David Roxan, the correspondent of that paper, had scrupulously respected my injunction as to the need for delicacy in presentation of the story. But, as many an M.P. has found to his cost, there is apparently no holding the headline writers! And here on the front page was the main feature story—M.P. APPEALS TO MESSINA— and, for good measure, heading the continuation of the story a few pages later, M.P. PLEADS TO SEE MESSINA.

This was early in 1959, well prior to the events depicted in my last chapter, but it was too much for my Carlisle friends just the same. It marked the end of the honeymoon period between myself and my supporters, which had lasted for some four years. It was made fairly clear to me by my Officers that, if I wanted to represent them at the next Election, I had best shut up about the Messinas: for the first time the disconcerting words fell upon my ears—I was 'alienating supporters'. (Though, since I increased my majority at the General Election six months later from 370 to 1998, I cannot have alienated as many as all that!)

My explanation that this was a matter which I was bringing up in the public interest was discountenanced. I had to think of the Party—and, of course (they added), the General Election.

I had probed on to the abscess which was already burrowing inwards to destroy the entire system and the patient had cried out aloud in agony and apprehension. For the conspiratorial society such as I have depicted in my Introduction has yet an additional complication. This is the undermining of society by the criminal conspirator, be he train robber, dope peddlar or foreign spy. For it is these days, eight years later, a truism to say that crime is no longer the simple thing that it was at one time, but it works by the clever trap, the ambush, the play on personal weakness, which may take many manifestations, yet always maintains the same overall devious form.

An *élite* in decay, such as we now consider, is particularly vulnerable to the criminal conspirator, for its sanctions against him are dated and outmoded—so outmoded that they sometimes still exist only in the imagination—owing to the failure to adjust them to new circumstances. The Law relating to Mental Health, which was the target of Norman Dodds* and myself during my first term at Westminster, depended on a much eroded Act of 1890. Even more important, the legislation on Chief Constables—which guaranteed these officers independence in their own balliwicks and freedom from supervision and control by the Home Secretary and Parliament, and which was under attack simultaneously by my colleague, Godfrey Lagden, Conservative M.P. for Hornchurch, and myself—hailed from the days of William IV in 1834. For many years, therefore, in the motoring age the criminals were endowed with a mobility denied to the law, until this was revised by Henry Brooke during his Home Secretaryship in 1964; and they took full advantage of that fact.

* The late Norman Dodds, Labour M.P. for Dartford, and subsequently Erith and Crayford, 1945–65.

But the decadent society maintains its vulnerability by maintaining its illusions—and its ire is reserved for those who endeavour to disturb these. Meanwhile, the conspiratorial society that is replacing it is of no help. To the members of this it is 'the conspiracy' that is all important even when by inadvertance it becomes entangled with the criminal conspiracy; it is always the individual who is its enemy, and he is treated as such, however hard he hollers.

'We will give him something to complain about,' says one of the civil service characters in C. P. Snow's *Corridors of Power* relative to such a complaining individual—and so, of course, they do.

However, these were not the sort of ideas that are even remotely acceptable to the leaders of a provincial Conservative Association, even if I had been able to think them up at short notice. So I shut up about Messina—until after the Election, anyway.

This was not easy. Throughout my last two chapters it may have been my complaint at times that I received insufficient attention by the Press. But not so now.

'Splendid publicity you've got!' greeted my ebullient friend, Norman Dodds, when I returned to Westminster the following week. The smile on Norman's face stretched from ear to ear. It had been his idea that I should announce that I was going to see Messina. It *was* a good idea: it had made the national headlines, as he predicted it would. But it was perhaps fortunate that Mr. Gino Messina (to whom I had, in fact, written) showed no desire to see me; and that the Belgian authorities, in whose charge he was at the time, put him over their frontier on the way to an unknown destination. Otherwise I cannot imagine what would have happened. Even so, I had my telephone ringing for weeks with calls from expectant Press representatives. It was too bad that I had to disappoint them. But it had been a close enough shave with the Association for the time being.

But now my lips can be unsealed. For it was the highly unusual experience, an experience which at the time it occurred lacked credibility, that coincided with the day that

I met Mr. Messina many years previously that coloured my outlook and sharpened my senses throughout my parliamentary life; making me hypersensitive to the forces of evil that seemed to hover in the background throughout the time during which my range of interest extended from an idiosyncratic experience in a country town until I became involved in the crisis precipitated by that equally strange affair in the high politics of the nation to which I am now endeavouring to give my special interpretation. This was some years before the manifestation on the national scene of that young lady even more famous than the Messina girls—Miss Christine Keeler.

The circumstances under which I met Mr. Messina had been well enough publicised: it was the incidental advantage of being a publisher that I had been able to do this. They formed the mainspring, both of a number of books—*Bars and Barricades, A Doctor Returns, Indian Hemp: A Social Menace, The Hallucinogenic Drugs, A Doctor in Parliament* (in part)— published during the 1950s (so many books that reviewers started to hint that I was becoming something of a bore); and also of my interest in the laws relating to mental illness.

In *Bars and Barricades* (published in 1952 and still available) I wrote the detail of this curious story, this event of phantasmagoric quality, which I can scarcely believe ever happened to me, were I not yet surrounded by friends and relatives, who are ready witnesses of the event. The record is there, however, in print over many years, of how, when taking over personally what was then our hotel (The Marlborough Arms, Woodstock, Oxfordshire), following a dispute with its manager, both Betty and I went into a disturbed state of mind and had to be removed and cared for, myself in hospital, Betty with her relatives—a rare 'double event' indeed for a previously normal couple, and one totally unknown, so I am assured by expert advisers, within the sphere of mental illness in so sudden a form as that which happened.

While Betty was hallucinating to the extent that, as she lay in the four-poster bed in Bedroom One, she continued to complain that the picture of *The Laughing Cavalier* on the wall was winking at her, I was loudly declaiming that I was the victim of a dope racket. Indeed, the medical certificate which removed me to hospital, copy of which I was later able to maintain, informs me that it was 'a sign of insanity' that I considered myself to have been doped.

This, admittedly, was long before the day when, as is the case now, heroin addicts in this country are increasing to such an extent that the rate is doubling in number every eighteen months and Britain is indicted by the United Nations Commission on Narcotic Drugs as having the highest rate of international drug trafficking—or even before it was disclosed in the Brain Report that doctors could freely and without hindrance prescribe, and did in some instances prescribe, vast amounts of heroin and morphia.* To have the idea that one was doped could in those days automatically have a bizarre quality to it. On the other hand, both Betty and I showed conspicuous signs of poisoning by atropine or some other hallucinogenic drug, as should have been obvious enough.

My imaginings (as *Bars and Barricades* records) went a good deal further than this and I was certain that 'the Russians, acting through their agents, had poisoned the bread and doped the wine so that the whole country was in danger'.

More absurd even than this was my particular belief, seemingly too ridiculous and out of place to put into a book written so soon after the event (although my eldest son, Christopher, at that time a freshman at Magdalen College and a spectator of this episode, still testifies to my proclaiming it) that, while dope was everywhere, it was in particular penetrating Oxford University. To this day, Christopher reminds me how he skilfully side-tracked my declared intention to go straight to the Vice-Chancellor and the Master of his College.

But this particular thesis is less ridiculous fifteen years later than it was in 1950. Following the tragic death of young Mr. Joshua Macmillan in early 1965, while an undergraduate at Oxford University, it leapt from phantasy into grim reality and became front page news.

* Interdepartmental Committee on Drug Addiction, Second Report H.M.S.O., 1965.

'We would welcome any concrete information we can get,' are the reported words of Dr. David Yardley, Senior Proctor of the University, in reference to the drug problem at Oxford. 'My C.I.D. officers are making enquiries,' declared Mr. C. G. Burrows, Chief Constable of Oxford.

Throughout the 1950s, however, the authorities in those parts did not show such enthusiasm for investigation in the face of my attempt to get enquiries started into the circumstances of the Johnson mishap. Accordingly, I had to be my own do-it-yourself C.I.D. as my abortive attempt to see Messina, already reported, and as my books, to which I have referred, offer full evidence.

But not even the books cover everything. Certain aspects inevitably remain unexplained in an incident such as this. In the course of my long investigation, things that at first appeared minor matters, suddenly leapt to the centre of the story when additional evidence came to hand. Unfortunately, when one is left to one's own resources as an investigator, such evidence may not come to hand until a very late stage in the proceedings.

In *Bars and Barricades* I report how, consequent on the crisis with our manager at the The Marlborough Arms Hotel, Betty and I started our hotel-keeping career 'at a very hot pace indeed' on a week-end of early October in 1950, surrounded (as I declared) 'by spies and conspirators'. Had I had space to particularise, I would have mentioned the hotel guest of foreign nationality—a regular visitor (so our staff told us) during the time that we had ourselves been living in London leaving the hotel in others' care—who had manifested himself with his lady to occupy our best bedroom with the four-poster bed (and the picture of *The Laughing Cavalier* on the wall) during the first week-end of our personal management. He was a distinguished member of a Foreign Embassy, so these simple people said (the Swiss Embassy, it was supposed to be), who was particularly interested in our former manager who was of that nationality.

If ostentatious display of wealth was anything of a criterion, they could well have been right—a large saloon car, white pigskin suitcases, expensive tailor-made foreign clothes, a haughty demand for special attention, were the conspicuous features of our new guest.

It came to Saturday evening, however, and our guest's air of distinction seemed to lapse. It is as if it were yesterday evening, and not more than fifteen years ago, that I can visualise his entering the door of the hotel bar leading in from the car park at 10.30 p.m. He had obviously been celebrating at a dinner party outside: this was in Oxford with our former manager, so my intelligence service informed me.

But something had outraged him, and it soon became clear what it was. It was the sight of my dear Betty, working behind the bar, clearing up and washing the mountain of glasses that had been left after closing time on a busy Saturday night. And in her mouth was—a cigarette—an inseparable companion on such occasions throughout the years I have known her.

'You allow your staff to smoke!" he upbraided me—and there was an aggressive glint in his eye. He drew himself up to his full height and swayed backwards and forwards on to his heels and off again.

'This is my wife,' I replied. 'This is our hotel and she can smoke if she wants to!' (This is the only known time when, as a husband, I have defended this habit.)

'I have employed one—hundred—girls', he swayed backwards and forwards, backwards and forwards as he emphasised the one hundred, 'and I have not at any time allowed them to smoke.' The glint became more aggressive.

By this time the conversation had reached an impasse. Our aggressive guest fortunately broke away and, muttering to himself, subsided into a chair in the lounge and then to bed. He left early next day with his large saloon car, his white pigskin suitcases and his blousy lady companion. I was not to see him again.

None the less, one does not readily forget so unusual an encounter. Particularly is this so when, within the space of a few days, one finds oneself going into a confused state such as I have described.

Who then *was* this man of the curious incident? I was to

seek him through the years, but find no single sign. The hotel register was totally uninformative as to the past: he was not to reappear in the future. It was as if he and his buxom companion had been wraiths. We sought him here: we sought him there. But he had vanished without trace. As, over the years, we endeavoured to make sense out of the strange happenings in Woodstock in October 1950, he was the Scarlet Pimpernel of the whole outfit.

It was only one evening in the month of October 1958, following eight years during which we had explored every avenue and left no stone unturned in our endeavours to solve the mystery story in which we were the central performers, as we were browsing through Betty's *Daily Mirror*, we saw this unforgettable face staring out from the page, recognisable after all these years, despite the dark glasses. The caption underneath the picture told us that here was Eugenio Messina, the well-known *souteneur* (procurer), who, following a prolonged trial in Brussels, had been sentenced by the Belgian authorities to six months imprisonment.

It needed only a small amount of further research to discover that this man was the most dynamic and the most notorious of the five Messina brothers, known as the managers of the 'Messina girls', who over the years had been the outstanding providers of the basic amenity of sex along the pavements of the West End of London.

A new and fascinating field of study opened up into the workings of this particular section of the underworld. Amongst my literary efforts, as I sat in the downstairs Interview Rooms' passage, was the editing of *The Men in My Life*, by Marthe Watts, the account of her life as a Messina girl. Throughout the war and the bombing of London, the Messina girls, like the Windmill Theatre, had 'never closed', but had carried on night after night, a highly disciplined army for the exploitation of sex, right through the war years and subsequently. A code of almost puritanical behaviour had governed their actions. When out in the streets they were not allowed to loll about against lamp posts or even walls; they had to wear high-necked dresses when 'on duty' and were not to expose themselves unnecessarily to clients; no client was allowed to stay more than ten minutes; above all, *they were not allowed to smoke.*

But what had happened in the meantime to the flamboyant Gino Messina, the *bon viveur*, the frequenter of select restaurants and the lounges of first-class hotels in Mayfair and Piccadilly— not to mention The Marlborough Arms at week-ends, where, so it seemed, he liked to free himself from business cares like the tycoon that he was, and spend a relaxed week-end with his strictly amateur mistress. Why could he no longer be found until he turned up in a Belgian courtroom eight years later?

The reason for this soon came to light. It is the first (in time) of the more notable coincidences which run through this book. For it so happened that the month of October 1950, when I had taken firm action in my own small world of The Marlborough Arms Hotel, Woodstock, had fortuitously coincided with a profound disturbance in the wider and more spacious world of Mr. Messina. It was at this identical time that *The People* had decided 'to blow the Messinas out of the water', so to speak, by featuring the late Duncan Webb's exposure of the gang's operations in the West End. London, hitherto a friendly city, had suddenly become a very hot place indeed for the Messinas. Gino had quickly removed himself to the Continent, living in Paris and Brussels: and London was to know him no more. Though the Messina girls carried on, as indeed they still do. For these hardy characters, surviving both newspaper 'exposure' and anti-prostitute legislation with the same aplomb as they survived the London blitz, still operate to-day as they have done over the years at what one might almost term 'a unique institution' at the address (which I do not propose to advertise) still being 're-exposed' by *The People* in 1964 and so continually familiar to the readers of that paper, which must presumably include the Chief Commissioner of Police at Scotland Yard. (Why this address should be the only one in London, as far as can be observed, that manages blatantly to advertise prostitution, it is impossible even to guess.) Once safely over the hurdle of the 1959 Election and back in Parliament again, I asked further questions about this address at the risk of my Carlisle Association Officers' continuing displeasure: but the result was a negative one. All I was doing was advertising the business: and there was little purpose in further action.

However, there is yet another sphere in which the remarkable Mr. Messina and his brothers can lay claim to fame. In his interesting book, *Dope International*,* Charles Wighton describes in his first chapter an incident (from information supplied by the American Federal Bureau of Narcotics) in which Eugenio Messina, with his brothers in minor roles, is shown as the central figure of a dope trafficking ring: the dope in question being that most profitable commodity of all—heroin. The form, as far as heroin is concerned, is that it makes its way westwards from where it is grown as opium in Turkey and Lebanon to the highly profitable market in the streets and dives of New York. It takes a devious path in transit, through Italy, through France, and also through Great Britain, changing hands from trafficker to trafficker on the way.

Dope and drugs? My own books on the subject that I have mentioned in this chapter, and other similar ones, must be consulted for full information.

It is enough for the moment to distinguish between heroin, morphia and the other opiates (so beneficial in their relief of pain on the one hand, so sinister and deleterious in their addictive use on the other) and the Indian hemp (marihuana) drugs—these latter being less injurious than the opiates in their harmful physical effects, but still possessing their strange hallucinating qualities which induce disturbed mental states.

Thus, when two people together, in the manner that Betty and I did at Woodstock in 1950, suddenly start to behave in wild and erratic fashion, and at the same time become victim to hallucinations, it is reasonable enough to say that they are poisoned by the hallucinogenic drugs—of which there are many vegetable and chemical varieties in addition to Indian hemp. They can be administered surreptitiously with the greatest of ease, say in a glass of sherry or other alcoholic beverage, and this can be done with graduated quantities

* *Dope International* by Charles Wighton (Frederick Muller, London, 1960).

with effects that vary from driving a person to temporary insanity with large doses to causing him merely to adopt an erratic pattern of behaviour in milder doses. Moreover, it is not impossible for poisoning by one drug to be used in order to defend trafficking in another and different drug.

It is at least a tenable hypothesis that we had inadvertently hit on a drug run being operated upon our own premises, and so had to be eliminated; even though my tenable hypothesis singularly failed to impress the police authorities on the spot. Unfortunately, however, my evidence, which I have set down so briefly in this chapter, has lain with them for many years, but I have not been aware of any enthusiasm to investigate it. As recently as October 1961 there was a Motion on the parliamentary paper in the following terms.

(Motion re Oxfordshire Constabulary)

That this House, appreciating the necessity for justice to the individual, uprightness in public administration and single-minded enforcement of the law, regrets the lack of alertness on the part of the Oxfordshire Constabulary in reference to certain events that took place in the Town of Woodstock, Oxfordshire, in October 1950 and the failure of the Chief Constable of Oxfordshire to investigate the reasonable suspicion of serious criminal activities on information supplied to him by the honourable Member for Carlisle, while at the same time deploring the lack of courtesy shown to the same Hon. Member in recent correspondence: and urges the immediate appointment of an Ombudsman or parliamentary commissioner responsible to parliament with powers to investigate and report publicly on complaints by individuals against administrative and executive authority.

This was signed not only by myself, but also by my Parliamentary colleagues, Henry Kerby and Harold Gurden, whom I had convinced by my evidence.

There with this Motion of 1961, and with the simultaneous

negative reply to me from the then Chief Constable of Oxfordshire, the late Mr. J. Bailey, we must leave this episode. After
going up hill and down dale, through parliamentary corridors
and through departments of government, I was at the end of
the road and could go no further.

★ ★ ★ ★ ★

There are, however, three reasons why my unhappy
adventure on the Day I Met Mr. Messina integrates into my
story.

First of all, this story speaks for itself of the lack of vigilence
of our society in the post-war years against the more unusual
forms of criminal conspiracy: it was just this fatal trait which
was eventually to destroy confidence in the Government of
Mr. Harold Macmillan.

Second, even though archaic legislation prevented me from
raising the events in Oxfordshire in 1950 directly in the House
of Commons during the time that I was an M.P.—until the
last few months of my stay in 1964 when more urgent matters
preoccupied me: I did, however, 'have a go' by raising all
associated matters whenever I could. I rang the bell of warning
over the threatening drug menace, which is now a reality,
acknowledged these days by the highest pundits to be the very
gravest of problems, whenever I could, through my books and
through Questions in the House. With, alas, the customary
negative results! ('Britain has no drug problem'—it is difficult
to imagine that this was the official slogan of only a few years
ago.) Let me give one example which I take from *Hansard*
of Thursday, 11th December 1958:

Oral Question, Number 3:

Dr. Donald Johnson: to ask the Secretary of State for
the Home Department, if he is aware of the dangerous
hallucinogenic properties of such new drugs as mescalin and
lysergic acid diethylamide: and when he proposes to bring
these drugs under the Dangerous Drugs Acts.

Mr. Butler: Yes, sir. I am informed that there is no

evidence that these drugs are addiction-producing; it would not, therefore, be appropriate to control them under the Dangerous Drugs Act, 1951.*

'What on earth is lysergic acid diethylamide?' queried my colleagues on the benches. They were right to ask. At the time my question was not even reported: it was to be some little while before lysergic acid diethylamide found fame as LSD, the menace drug, a single grain of which can cause complete loss of mental balance. It was almost *eight* years before the Home Office awoke from its slumbers to do something and, it was finally on the day before these words are written, 21st July 1966, that the announcement comes from Mr. Roy Jenkins, Home Secretary, that this and similar drugs are to be controlled under the Drugs (Prevention of Misuse) Act. Appearing on TV a day or two later, Mr. Roy Jenkins asked for information: I am sending him a copy of this book.

Third, last but not least, an experience such as I have described cannot but endow one with a measure of insight. To be the victim of 'a mixed-up conspiracy' gives one an unusual point of view.

In my opening words to this book, I have compared our era to that of the Renaissance and I do not think I am far wrong. We are back to the Borgias, indeed, dealing in our conspiratorial society with a whole new class of potent and poisonous drugs of unusual and devious action.

As the German toxicologist, Lewis Lewin, has shown in his book, *Der Gifte in der Weltgeschichte* (J. Springer, Berlin, 1920), this class of drugs in their more primitive form have flitted in and out of world history since Classical times as poisoning agents, whether for use in personal vendettas or as instruments of policy. For instance, it is more than likely that the oracle at Delphi, whose utterances were so profoundly revered throughout the Ancient World, yet on occasions so obscure, must have been produced by some such means: the chroniclers report that the state of mind of the priestess was induced by 'a mephitic vapour'.

* *Hansard*: Vol. 597, Column 485.

These drugs are drugs of confusion. The reactions of the poisoned persons are those of intense fear and apprehension at one moment, intense mirth and euphoria the next, when it is as if the jester God of G. K. Chesterton has taken over the firmament, the God of Humour, of strange and meaningless coincidence, of ludicrous associations that show proud mankind to be merely the plaything of a capricious destiny. Above all, the effect on the victim is that he renders himself ridiculous and, by becoming a laughing stock, is led to destruction.

There are large gaps in our knowledge. Can a whole *élite* be slowly poisoned in this way so that they exhibit such symptoms? It makes an interesting speculation. Who can say that this is entirely impossible in days such as these?—and with drugs such as LSD added to the poisoner's armoury.

'The British have many of the irrational physical and psychological reactions symptomatic of drug takers', states the American psychologist, Mr. William Schlackmann, in an interview reported in the *Daily Telegraph* on 23rd July 1966. But he is merely talking of the lower classes and tea.

I can only report my own personal reactions, as perhaps sensitised by a unique experience: and at the same time report the events of the final months of the Macmillan Government as faithfully as I can, while leaving the reader to form his own conclusions.

Thus, starting with the first of these, I have to record that, while for the overwhelming majority of my existence—that is to say, for some 99.9 per cent of the time—I am able to survey the scene around me with an equable temperament and view it in its normal coherent form and shape, there have been other brief occasions when it has been as if an earthquake has hit this solid structure of the surrounding world, cracks and rents have appeared (metaphorically speaking) in the earth beneath my feet, and vast holes have gaped endangering my whole position in life. Unusual coincidences have started to happen, then these coincidences have formed a pattern: suddenly, as the pattern has started to manifest itself, I am living a James Bondish type of existence, struggling with evil forces that threaten to engulf me.

I make no further explanation of this. I merely state it as a fact that, on the two or three interludes in an otherwise prosaic and uneventful existence when it has occurred, this has been when I was in the position of either finding out too much, or perhaps asking too many questions, when I was adjacent, through no particular fault of my own, to such forces as those which I have described.

One such occasion was when my course in life collided with that curious amalgam of ministerial indiscretion and erratic sex behaviour, the Profumo-Ward-Keeler affair. This particular experience had, however, one quite unique feature: it was that the coincidences of which I have to talk did not solely concern me personally, but comprehended a wide range of event beyond my personal affairs.

CHAPTER TEN

OTHER WINDS OF CHANGE

(1)

No COMPREHENSIVE consideration of the Profumo affair
can be contained within the context of politics alone.
Any book attempting to do this would rightly be
regarded as a disappointing document.

During the 1950s, coincident with the political and economic
revolution, at the head of which Mr. Harold Macmillan had
put himself in so flamboyant a fashion, there was the sex
revolution introducing the new morality, whose manifestations
are that much more familiar in everyday life than is any
political factor. Indeed, it is ironical that the skilful political
juggler of The Wind of Change should finally have been
brought down by a backlash of that other contemporary
revolution. What better evidence could one wish of the
monastic seclusion in which British parliamentary life is lived?

Let us think, in turn, of the 'new morality' in a wider
context than that of young people hopping into bed with
each other prior to marriage amidst the comments of disapproving clergymen (or even, on occasions, acclaiming
clergymen) or of the much-publicised four-letter word on the
B.B.C.; or of occasional simple adultery.

We must, therefore, leave the minor personal incidents of
the new morality to the publicity-seeking prelates, both con
and pro; the victorious dissemination of Anglo-Saxon mono-
syllables to the more prurient publishers; the trivialities of
misbehaviour of the plebs to The People newspaper; and browse
for a while in that no-man's-land between sex and politics

which has been so little studied and yet which has far more significance for good or ill than the millions of words of libertarian sex writing that has appeared in papers, magazines and books throughout the years.

Whether the era is a puritanical one for sex customs or whether it is libertarian, there are few nations less happy in the conduct of relationships between the sexes than the British. We are rightly considered by our Continental friends to be a nation of muddlers in dealing with those fundamental problems which they on their side solve comparatively so well, but in which we are bogged down, if not by puritanism and native inhibitions, than by political sentimentality, bogus psychology and left-wing progressive nostrums. At the moment, for better or worse, we enjoy the libertarian attitude to sex, but this too has brought its problems and has had, also, to be interpreted in terms of the rise of aggressive feminism. Delving into the history of the last hundred years, one is almost led to believe that the segregation of the sexes which is so prominent a characteristic of British upper- and middle-class life has been embarked upon as a policy of desperation.

Even in this day and age, the basic features of this segregation remain in the institutions of our Establishment. Nowhere, perhaps, is this more conspicuous than in the life of the House of Commons—ask the wife of any Member of Parliament, if you wish corroboration of this.

What can a Parliamentary wife do within the precincts of the House of Commons other than sit in the public entertainment room (Harcourt Room), in the Strangers' Dining Room or in an uncomfortable seat in the Strangers' Gallery? The effect being to ensure briefness and sparsity of visits—and a segregation of the inmates from the female sex reminiscent of one of Her Majesty's even more rigorous penal institutions. Nor can the entrance of women M.P.s, splendid as is their contribution in other ways, be said to have ameliorated this position.

Throughout British history, in contrast to the French experience, except perhaps for a brief time during the reign of Charles II, romance and the exercise of power politics have been strangers to each other: wives of kings and statesmen have been ciphers in the historical process, mistresses mere playthings. What more inevitable than that, on those rare occasions when the barrier between politics and sex has been penetrated, the mixture has been an explosive one, whether it be the vicissitudes of King George IV and Queen Caroline, the romance of Parnell and Kitty O'Shea, or the adventures of Sir John Dilke? It is to this unfortunate tradition that the brief love affair of John Profumo and Christine Keeler belongs.

British statesmen throughout the centuries have not been notable at all times for their virtuous way of life, but the traditional *élite*, however they may have laid themselves open to criticism in other ways, can, at least, be credited with having created a stable social system. As a part of the rigid class structure, there was the *monde*, and the *demi-monde*. The latter provided its comforts and conveniences but, beyond that, it was securely kept in its place, where it could not interfere in any way with good government or, trained in discretion as it was, with the personal reputations of those who frequented it.

It is probably no coincidence that those who have sponsored the revolution in sex morals are, by and large, of the same political faith as those who wish to disrupt traditional society from an economic and political point of view. Amongst other things, there is the inexplicable contradiction in the arguments of the progressive sex warrior. He will advocate the virtues of sex education for children in their early teens, the beneficial effect of incontinence amongst the young, easy divorce, the necessity for legalisation of abortion and of homosexual acts between consenting adults: but, coming to the prostitute (who is the ally of stability inasmuch as she copes discreetly with the endemic problem of excessive male desire), she is 'out'. Biological facts are turned inside out to fit in with such contradictory arguments as these. They do, however, have a common factor in that one and all make for the disruption of traditional bourgeois society.

For, with the suppression of the prostitute—an almost total elimination in the West End of London since the passing of the Street Offences Act, 1959, with the possible exception of the premises owned by Mr. Messina—there has appeared the 'model', this polymorphous young lady of highly dubious social pedigree. The changes of social life have provided fertile ground for the rise of 'the model'. By the early post-war years the exclusive world of private entertaining with its strictly controlled etiquette had been replaced by the chromium plate and continental restaurateur society, in which high and low, socialite and criminal, could mingle chummily together in the latest fashionable eating 'place of worship' of a materialistic age. Thus, whereas the prostitute had been rigidly excluded from polite society, the 'model', whatever manifestation she took, became a classless symbol of the new age, clothed with a bogus respectability, escalating upwards or moving downwards in the social scale with glorious abandon, now with the best, now with the worst. Such a one as this was Miss Christine Keeler—the young woman from the caravan estates who not only achieved contemporary fame, but who may well live in history as a Joan of Arc of the sex revolution.

All this was a different society indeed from the cloistered world of the House of Commons, still set in its nineteenth-century ways, out of touch, both collectively and severally, with the nation which it had set itself to govern. But this was a dynamic and ruthless society which, human nature being what it is and not all members of any legislative body being of monkish mould, could not indefinitely be kept at bay from the seat of government. Indeed, it became the Achilles heel of Conservative Government, so impregnable in all other ways.

*   *   *   *   *

I do not represent either Conservative Ministers or Conservative M.P.s as being monsters of vice presiding over a dissolute society. The truth, which is rather to the contrary, must be set on record quickly before misapprehensions are handed down to future generations. I have already referred to the remoteness of the parliamentary atmosphere from real life in the days of the Old Establishment. Here they were, secure in their own world: naïve, old-fashioned people living in a surviving enclave of Edwardian society, bounded by their fields and their country estates on the one hand, their protected life within the safe battlements of the Party machine on the other, sheltered from impact with the outside world by their own exclusive way of life.

To return to my simile of an earlier chapter: as one gazed across from the counterscarp, the rugged fortifications loomed up to the sky, as impregnable as ever against those who aspired to enter by frontal attack. Yet who would have thought that the foundations were so eroded that the whole edifice was to collapse into dust and even a year or two later be 'one with Nineveh and Tyre'? For it was not the enemy at the gates, but the gnawing of the sewer rats below that finally brought it to ruin.

The commander of the garrison stood proudly on the summit of the keep, surrounded by his fiercely glaring lieutenants, heedless and contemptuous of the sea of mud and slime that was rising to engulf him, waving aside in his vanity all attempts to warn him of disaster. Yet he too was soon to go—though, alas, not quite soon enough to save the citadel.

'Of course I was deceived,' declared Mr. Harold Macmillan, relative to the Profumo situation in his final speech in the House of Commons on the Debate on Security and the Denning Report on 16th December 1963.

But why?

As far as the last years of the Macmillan reign were concerned, the Profumo case did not exist in isolation. There had been the dreary sequence of spy cases. Burgess and Maclean. Lonsdale and the Krogers. Henry Houghton and Miss Gee. Blake. Vassall. So went on the sorry tale of traitors, discovered in most cases too late.

There seemed no limit to the gullibility of the British people, or of their appointed guardians. Or perhaps I should say 'of the English people', as I made the distinction in the Supplementary Question which I asked the Prime Minister, following my own Question to him on 22nd June 1961, subsequent to the Romer Report on the Portland spy case (and two years before the Profumo scandal), as to whether he would issue a warning on security-mindedness. This was my Supplementary Question:

Is there not a general lesson in this Report that we English are a simple-minded people who are easily deceived, that we live in the past when wars were fought according to conventions, rules and protocols? As one who, like him, has Scottish crofter ancestors, may I ask the Prime Minister whether he will bring an element of Scottish shrewdness to the consideration of this matter.*

Such questions as this were considered irrelevancies. But I was by no means the only person imparting warnings. According to the *Daily Mail* of 2nd February 1966, Commander Anthony Courtney, then M.P. for Harrow East, with two Conservative colleagues, had warned Mr. Harold Macmillan against the state of the security system as far back as 1959. They were assured by the Prime Minister that 'the Government did not lack vigilance'.

Can we afford to be deceived? Can we afford to deceive ourselves? Can we afford to have those in charge of our affairs who allow themselves to be deceived?

Of course we cannot.

In contrast to the British way of sex with its blundering habits, its sloppy thinking, its sentimentalities and its contradictions, is the Russian way of sex, hard and clear—sex with the hidden camera, love and its curiosities on the microfilm. All stored away for use at a suitable moment.

In the modern age it is goodbye to the wars fought with battalions and battleships. The cold war is no longer fought on the high seas or the open plains, but in the hotel bedrooms and the night clubs of the large cities, while its weapons are sex scandal, blackmail and the destruction of reputations. Those who may have scoffed at this at the time of which I write (and my public warning to the Prime Minister was accompanied by other and more specific warnings to authorities behind the scenes) can do so no longer since the sensational

* *Hansard*: Vol. 642, Column 1686.

case of Commander Anthony Courtney, the former M.P. whom I have just mentioned.

A particularly dangerous enemy of the Russians, Commander Courtney found himself seriously embarrassed by the distribution of compromising photographs, taken in a Moscow hotel bedroom, to his constituency chairman and to other people of political importance. A bluff and hearty campaigner, the Commander performed a notable service by fighting this out with his constituency officers. But how many other distinguished people have been successfully compromised in similar fashion? How many other cases may there have been (beside that of the traitor, Vassall) where suitable blackmail might have been paid to buy off such a fate? We do not know. Bravery and physical courage may well have been our sterling quality to bring us victory in previous wars, but now a different set of tenets apply: in the existing cold war our principal enemy is our own gullibility.

In a society in which the simplest tricks can, first of all, deceive the whole panoply of authority, then subsequently have the effect of authority rallying round, ostensibly in its own support, but in actual fact in support of crime itself, there are no limits to the dividends that simple deceit, carried off with a measure of aplomb, might bring.

I cannot do better than quote Paragraphs 4 to 6 of the 'Summary of The Main Findings of the Romer Committee' published in *Hansard* of 13th June 1961 in respect of the Portland Spy Case, in which Henry Houghton and his lady friend, Ethel Gee, were found guilty of supplying secret information to Gordon Lonsdale and the Krogers:

> 4. In 1954, an allegation was made to a junior official who was Houghton's immediate superior in the small section of the Underwater Detection Establishment in which Houghton worked that the latter was taking secret papers out of the Establishment. This official did not report the matter or take any other steps in regard to it apart from advising his informant to see the Security Officer or the police and he is very much to blame for his inaction.

5. In 1956, Houghton was twice brought to the notice of the authorities in the Underwater Detection Establishment as a probable security risk. Insufficient investigations were made and a report which was both incomplete and misleading was submitted to the Admiralty. The Security Officer at the Establishment is gravely to blame for the casual way in which he dealt with this matter. Even so, the Captain of the Establishment should personally have ensured that proper inquiries were conducted and that the matter was fully reported to the Admiralty.

6. The main responsibility for the failure to make a proper investigation of Houghton in 1956 rests, therefore, with the authorities in the Underwater Detection Establishment at that time. The evidence discloses that there was a general want of 'security mindedness' in the Establishment; and responsibility for this must rest with the Captain of the Establishment. But the Admiralty, and the Security Service, although they received only an incomplete and misleading report from Portland, cannot escape criticism for failing to press the matter to a positive conclusion.*

Similar attitudes prevailed in the other notorious spy cases of the time. It is merely that the excellent Sir Charles Romer did not pull his punches in his comments and did not allow himself to be one of the 'whitewash' brigade.

In fact, it will be recollected that Henry Houghton, the convicted person in the Portland case, was a man who cut quite a dash. He was able to do this with the help of the money which he obtained from espionage. Far from this making him suspect, however, the prestige of being seen in the right places as a good spender appeared to endow him with immunity to suspicion. Indeed it came out at the trial that, when his wife reported to the authorities, in the manner mentioned by Sir Charles Romer, that he was taking secret papers home to read, this complaint was dismissed merely as the act of a jealous woman.

Let us glance briefly at the unfortunate series of Mr. Harold

* *Hansard*: Vol. 642, Columns 216, 217.

Macmillan's accident-prone Ministers. Even with those undoubtedly above suspicion of sexual vagaries: each case, in its turn, in its several way—Galbraith and Vassall, Fletcher-Cooke and the young man who had borrowed his car—has the strange appearance of a frame-up. Indeed, a familiar pattern manifests itself. It was as if the victims, caught unaware, were turned to ridicule far beyond the measure of their offence.

Did nobody bother to investigate these cases as a pattern? It would seem not. For it remained for the irresponsible Profumo to fall into the slimiest pit of all.

(2)

In ascertaining further the nature of the threat against which Mr. Harold Macmillan, as Head of the Security Services, failed to defend the country and of the trap into which John Profumo fell, rather than risk any charge of bias and exaggeration, I am best relying upon Lord Denning's Report which was published in September 1963. I cannot in any case better the words of the relevant paragraphs.

Before I do this, however, it is important for me to remind my readers once again of the full context in which the Profumo case occurred. It was, let me emphasise again, one of a multitude in which Russian conspiracy proved itself successful. Following even the early revelations of spy cases it was the bounden duty of all to be vigilant during these years. For few people in prominent positions, such as Members of Parliament, escaped the attentions of the Soviet Embassy or the embassies of its ideological companion countries.

Such attentions could take a variety of forms, according to the chosen subject's interests or susceptibilities—or, of course, his potential use. Though for the average M.P., who is probably rated rather low in the scale, the initial approach is one of unimpeachable austerity. (For the political journalist on the other hand, the bait can be a slap-up luncheon at a fashionable restaurant, though Ian Waller of the *Sunday Telegraph* tells me that, even so, one quickly finds oneself downgraded both as to fare and place of entertainment, if one fails to respond suitably to this initial burst of generosity.)

For such as I, it merely took the form of invitations to Chinese Red Cross functions (it needed three refusals before I was dropped from the list of invitees), to the Soviet Embassy to see a space-flight film or to one of the latter's offshoots in South Kensington to meet a party of journalists and editors. At such festive occasions one would be encouraged in slightly gauche manner to expand on one's own interests in Parliament —an irresistible request to the majority of politicians. Indeed, it was a slightly uncanny sensation to find each of one's hosts after the other making this their opening conversational gambit. Should one be unresponsive to these ordinary blandishments, it was only a question of time before one became the target of higher talent in the shape of a charming, and open-minded conversationalist, who would drop the hint of continuing this enjoyable acquaintance over lunch one day— but perhaps one would be along to see another film at the Embassy in the meantime?

But this was as far as I personally graduated. My own luncheon never materialised. For the next Soviet Embassy film to which I was invited was on a Friday night, the night for our bourgeois family enjoyment at the end of the parliamentary week, when a star film at our local cinema proved a greater attraction: and, after that, I received no more invitations. Clearly, rebel though I might be, I lacked the necessary *angst* to make anything of a defector.

Surely, with *all* Members of Parliament, even the most unlikely ones such as myself, being liable to such approaches, no prominent person can conduct himself too circumspectly in a time of cold war.

★　　★　　★　　★　　★

The following are the extracts from Lord Denning's Report:

CHAPTER I: THE PRINCIPAL PERSONS

(i) *Stephen Ward*

10. The story must start with Stephen Ward, aged 50. The son of a clergyman, by profession he was an osteopath with consulting rooms at 38 Devonshire Street, W.1. His skill was

very considerable and he included among his patients many well-known people. He was also an accomplished portrait artist. His sitters included people of much eminence.

He had a quick and easy manner of conversation which attracted some, but repelled others. It pleased him much to meet people in high places, and he was prone to exaggerate the nature of his acquaintanceships with them. He would speak of many of them as if they were great friends when, more often than not, he had only treated them as patients or drawn their portraits.

11. Yet he was at the same time utterly immoral. He had a small house or flat in London at 17 Wimpole Mews, W.1, and a country cottage on the Cliveden Estate next to the River Thames. He used to pick up pretty girls of the age of 16 or 17, often from night clubs, and induce them to come and stay with him at his house in London. He used to take these girls down at week-ends to his cottage. He seduced many of these himself. He also procured them to be mistresses for his influential friends.

He did not confine his attention to promiscuity. He catered also for those of his friends who had perverted tastes. There is evidence that he was ready to arrange for whipping and other sadistic performances. He kept collections of porno-graphic photographs. He attended parties where there were sexual orgies of a revolting nature.

In money matters he was improvident. He did not keep a banking account. He got a firm of solicitors to keep a sort of banking account for him, paying in cheques occasionally to them and getting them to pay his rent. More often he cashed his incoming cheques through other people; or paid his bills with the incoming cheques. He had many cash transactions which left no trace.

12. Finally, he admired the Soviet régime and sympathised with the Communists. He used to advocate their cause in conversation with his patients, so much so that several became suspicious of him. With others he was more discreet. He became very friendly with a Russian, Captain Eugene Ivanov. To him I now turn.

(ii) *Eugene Ivanov*

13. Captain Eugene Ivanov was an assistant Russian Naval
Attaché at the Russian Embassy in London. As such his role
would be diplomatic only. He came to this country on 27th
March 1960. But the Security Service discovered that he was
also a Russian Intelligence Officer. He had qualities not
normally found in a Russian officer in this country. His
English was reasonably good and he was able to converse
easily. He drank, however, a good deal and was something
of a ladies' man.

He was keen to meet people in this country. He was very
impressed by persons of title, particularly peers of the realm.
He lost no opportunity of advocating the Russian viewpoint.
He was, according to Stephen Ward, 'an absolutely dedicated
Communist and also a nice person'. And he was quite open
about his position. Right from the start he would tell his
hearers, 'Anything you say goes back to Moscow. Look out
what you say'.

14. Stephen Ward and Captain Ivanov became great friends.
Captain Ivanov was often down at the cottage at Cliveden
at week-ends. He visited Stephen Ward's house in London.
They met in restaurants. They often played bridge together.
Stephen Ward introduced him to many of his friends, both
those of high rank and also the girls. And Stephen Ward lost
no opportunity of helping him, as the events show.

15. It has been suggested to me that Ivanov filled a new role
in Russian technique. It was to divide the United Kingdom
from the United States by these devious means. If Ministers
or prominent people can be placed in compromising situations,
or made the subject of damaging rumour, or the Security
Service can be made to appear incompetent, it may weaken
the confidence of the United States in our integrity and
reliability.

So a man like Captain Ivanov may take every opportunity
of getting to know Ministers or prominent people—not so
much to obtain information from them (though this would be
a useful by-product)—but so as to work towards destroying

confidence. If this were the object of Captain Ivanov with Stephen Ward as his tool he succeeded only too well.

(Ivanov was Captain 2nd Rank in the U.S.S.R. Navy, equivalent to Commander in the Royal Navy.)

(iii) *Christine Keeler*

16. Christine Keeler is a girl, now aged 21, whose home is at Wraysbury. She left home at the age of 16 and went to London. She was soon employed at the Murray Cabaret Club as a show-girl which involved, as she put it, just walking around with no clothes on.

She had only been at the Cabaret Club a short time when Stephen Ward came there and they danced together. Thereafter he often telephoned her and took her out. After a very few days he asked her to go and live with him. She went. She ran away from him many times but she always went back. He seemed to control her. She lived with him at 17 Wimpole Mews from about June 1961 to March 1962.

He took her to his country cottage at Cliveden and he introduced her to many men, sometimes men of rank and position, with whom she had sexual intercourse. (A jury has since found him guilty on a charge of living on the earnings of her prostitution.) She had undoubted physical attractions. Later on, he introduced her also to the drug Indian hemp and she became addicted to it. She met coloured men who trafficked in it and she went to live with them.

(iv) *Lord Astor*

21. Lord Astor got to know Stephen Ward in 1950 when he went to him as a patient after a fall at hunting. Stephen Ward treated him well and cured him. Ever since that time Lord Astor had sent him many of his friends as patients.

22. In 1955 Lord Astor let Stephen Ward a cottage on the Cliveden Estate. The cottage was down by the river, while the big house is on top of the hill. To get from the cottage to the house it is a quarter to half a mile's steep walk, or one mile by road.

Stephen Ward used to come at week-ends and give osteo-pathic treatment to Lord Astor and those of his guests who desired it. The account, including payment for the guests was charged to Lord Astor. Stephen Ward often had visitors at this cottage. Usually they came for the day and remained down at the cottage. When Stephen Ward went to the big house to give treatment he went by himself. On occasions, Lord Astor invited him to come up to Cliveden for lunch or for drinks.

23. Lord Astor had no sympathy with Stephen Ward's political views and made it clear to him. But at the pressing request of Stephen Ward, he did on occasions help him in approaching the Foreign Office (as will appear later) but not in any way sponsoring his views.

24. Lord Astor has helped Stephen Ward with money from time to time. In 1952, when Stephen Ward was starting, not yet established in practice, Lord Astor lent him £1250, which Stephen Ward repaid over the succeeding years by professional services. And Lord Astor has on occasion advanced sums to him since, on the understanding that it was an advance to be repaid by expenses of treatment.

In May 1963 Stephen Ward opened a banking account and Lord Astor guaranteed an overdraft up to £1500. This was because Stephen Ward anticipated legal expenses and also desired to acquire premises for an office and residence. All the receipts from his practice and elsewhere were to go towards repayment.

CHAPTER II—THE CLIVEDEN WEEK-END

(ii) *Mr. Profumo's Association with Christine Keeler*

30. It is apparent that during this week-end Mr. Profumo was much attracted by Christine Keeler and determined to see her again, if he could. This was, of course, easy, through Stephen Ward. In the next few days and weeks Mr. Profumo made assignations with Christine Keeler. He visited her at

Stephen Ward's house and had sexual intercourse with her there. Sometimes he called at a time when Stephen Ward or if someone else was there. He would then take her for a drive until the coast was clear.

On one occasion he did not use his own car because his wife had it in the country. He used a car belonging to a Minister which had a mascot on it. He drove her to see Whitehall and Downing Street, also Regent's Park. Mr. Profumo wrote two or three notes to Christine Keeler and gave her one or two presents such as perfume and a cigarette lighter. She said her parents were badly off and he gave her £20 for them, realising that this was a polite way on her part of asking for money for her services.

In August 1961, whilst his wife was in the Isle of Wight, he took Christine Keeler to his own house in Regent's Park. Altogether I am satisfied that his object in visiting her was simply because he was attracted by her and desired sexual intercourse with her.

It has been suggested that Captain Ivanov was her lover also. I do not think he was. The night of Sunday, 9th July 1961, was an isolated occasion. I think Captain Ivanov went to Stephen Ward's house for social entertainment and conversation and not for sexual intercourse.

I do not believe that Captain Ivanov and Mr. Profumo ever met in Stephen Ward's house or in the doorway. They did, no doubt, narrowly miss one another on occasions; and this afforded Stephen Ward and Christine Keeler much amusement. (Later on, a great deal has been made of this episode. It has been suggested that Captain Ivanov and Mr. Profumo were sharing her services. I do not accept this suggestion.)

(iii) *The Request for Information*

31. About this time, probably during the Cliveden week-end, Captain Ivanov told Stephen Ward that the Russians knew as a fact that the American Government had taken a decision to arm Western Germany with atomic weapons, and he asked Ward to find out through his influential friends when this

decision was to be implemented. Without saying so in so many words, Captain Ivanov with some subtlety implied that, if Stephen Ward supplied the answer, his trip to Moscow would be facilitated.

(3)

It is only fair that Miss Christine Keeler should have the last word in this chapter. Speaking from the wisdom of twenty-one years old about her former friend, John Profumo, she made the following comment in the course of a statement given to reporters of the *Sunday Pictorial* and reproduced in the Denning Report:

'I believe that a man in his position should not indulge in pastimes like me. I suppose even Ministers are only human, but I think that they should curb their feelings when they take on the job.

'One might think that, as a politician, he would have been particularly discreet in the affair. John Profumo was not.'

CHAPTER ELEVEN

A GAME OF GOLF

HERE THEN was the pit so ably described by Lord Denning. The tantalising question opens up: was this set-up a fortuitous one, or was it a carefully planned and cunningly contrived booby-trap in which, once the victim was enmeshed, he sank deeper into the mire in whichever direction he trod?

For, if it had been hoped that the Profumo statement in the House of Commons on 22nd March 1963 would dispel rumour and allay suspicion, it signally failed in this.

Apart from those at Westminster or in Fleet Street who had some intimate knowledge of detail, the popular newspapers had already said sufficient to whet the appetite for scandal throughout the country and though, of course, few had full knowledge of the circumstances so comprehensively described at a later date by Lord Denning, there was enough piecemeal knowledge available for rumour to build up and so to inflame the sex complexes and the neuroses of an entire nation. The libel threat by Profumo, for instance, threw no mantle of protection over Miss Christine Keeler: and the exotic speculations that surrounded her and her friend and fellow Ward-girl, Miss Mandy Rice-Davies, developed into a latter-day cult of Aphrodite.

Temporarily subdued though the British papers might be by threat of libel, there was still the excitement of the American and Continental papers appearing with torn-out pages and the natural speculation as to what these missing pages had contained. While, as the spring of 1963 progressed, the fervour spread to the Continent of Europe. *La belle Christine* took prior

place for week after week in the peep-show of British affairs
presented to the French nation by those papers whose circula-
tion depends on the production of never-ending scandalous
stories of British high society for the delectation of an egalitarian
people. Co-featuring was, of course, *le docteur Ward*. While
charabancs from distant Hamburg crowded the austere
purlieus of Harley Street for their passengers to enjoy a glimpse
of the famous flat in Devonshire Street, the abode of the god-
dess, thus disrupting the smooth running of more than one
medical establishment through the curiosity aroused amongst
the staff.

It was scarcely to be expected that, in this atmosphere of
delirium, fine distinctions should be made between those who
patronised the versatile Doctor Ward in one of his capacities
and those who patronised him in another: though there is no
reason whatever to disbelieve those distinguished figures who
had patronised him as a portrait painter, or indeed as an
osteopath, when they denied knowledge of the more sinister
side of his character. None the less, there was something of the
aspect of a French farce about the situation when (as is confirmed by Lord Denning) so respected a figure of the Establishment as Sir Godfrey Nicholson, Conservative M.P. for
Farnham, was known to have recommended Stephen Ward's
talents to almost half his Conservative colleagues in the House
of Commons. For Stephen Ward had made monkeys out
of everyone within range and the situation was a bonanza for
the young team of satirical impresarios on BBC television,
That Was The Week That Was, amongst whom the political
Establishment had already been the target of humour for a
year or more.

Amidst the aphrodisiac excitement, the vast majority of
people seemed to miss the real point of the situation. Amongst
my news-cuttings of that time I find only one that states this.
This is Hugh Massingham's article in the *Sunday Telegraph* of
24th March 1963:

'Mr Profumo's private life is not important. What matters
is the revelation that an official of the Russian Embassy—

an official who is almost certainly a member of the Soviet
Intelligence Service—had penetrated so far into high
society.'

The writer shows further prescience with his comment that
'Mr. Profumo's statement cannot be the end of the affair.
We are at the beginning of something and no one at this stage
can say where it will lead us.'

In this article too there is the first public mention of the
state of Mr. Harold Macmillan's health. For Mr. Hugh
Massingham continues:

'. . . it is another instance of the Prime Minister's extraordinary lack of judgment. Watching him while he listened
to Mr. Profumo's statement on Friday morning, Labour
Members noticed Mr. Macmillan's worn, exhausted look,
and wondered how long he could continue, now that the
difficulties are piling up with every day that passes. Nor
should we assume that it is merely love of power that keeps
him where he is. He cannot leave us now even if that was
his dearest wish. For the sake of the Government and Party
he leads, he must stay and face the music.

'Really Ministers have only themselves to blame. They
drift. They allowed the Galbraith rumours to go on and on
in the hope, one must suppose, that something, somehow,
would turn up to save them . . .'

★   ★   ★   ★   ★

That 'something would turn up' had become the philosophy
of Macmillan Government. Any difficulty was 'the little local
difficulty' which—whether it be the resignation of Lord
Salisbury, or that of Peter Thorneycroft or Enoch Powell,
or the indiscretion of Profumo—could be played down. It
would shrink in size and, hey presto, finally disappear.

But in the spring and summer of 1963 difficulties did not
disappear. Luck, that essential political commodity of which
throughout my own generation the Conservative Party had

seemed to have an inexhaustible fund, now seemed in short supply. For the Profumo-Christine Keeler scandal had no sooner 'blown' than towards the end of April there appeared the report of the Radcliffe Tribunal on the Vassall case. Here is comment from *The Times* editorial columns on 26th April concerning this:

'The history of Vassall as a spy falls into two phases. The Tribunal find that the system by which he was selected for duty in the British Embassy in Moscow was inadequate and that he was obviously a very bad choice for service in a sensitive post behind the Iron Curtain. They are, however, curiously reticent in their conclusions about the circumstances in which he was suborned by intelligence agents without apparently arousing any serious suspicion in the Embassy. The Naval Attaché, Captain Bennett, was evidently dissatisfied with Vassall and suspected him of being a latent homosexual. He communicated his concern to Sir William Hayter, the British Ambassador to the Admiralty and to his successor as Naval Attaché. Yet nothing happened and subsequently Captain Bennett, clearly ashamed of his suspicions, was able to write a glowing confidential report on Vassall.

'Later, an Embassy typist supplied information suggesting that a Russian employee at the Embassy was a Soviet agent and that Vassall was on his list of "targets". Although this information was passed to the acting Head of Chancery in a minute from the Military Attaché "the history of action taken on the minute", to use the rather gnomic language of the Report, "is obscure". In more direct terms it appears that nothing was done about it. In the light of these disclosures it is surprising to read the Tribunal's view that the general security system in the Embassy was sound and well maintained.

'The second phase of Vassall's espionage was in the Admiralty itself. The explanation advanced by the Tribunal for Vassall's success in removing secret documents for six years without arousing the suspicions of two or three colleagues who shared his office is that each individual was concentrated on his own work at his desk—an image of application to duty which surely overestimates the industry of the most conscientious Admiralty clerk. Perhaps the most disturbing aspect of the whole affair is that of Vassall's "positive vetting". This form of security screening, designed for people having regular and constant access to Top Secret defence information or material, was applied to Vassall soon after his return from Russia. Yet the investigation carried out partly by the Admiralty and partly by the Ministry of Supply was completed without direct reference to anyone who had supervision over Vassall or worked closely with him during the whole of his two years in Moscow. This extraordinary lapse is treated by the Tribunal as no more than an error of judgment; they conclude that positive vetting was carried out in accordance with pre-scribed procedure.'

And so on and so on. More or less coincident with this, on 23rd April 1963, I was amongst seven parliamentary questioners enquiring of the Prime Minister as to whether he is satisfied with the present state of the security organisations, consequent in the dissemination of secret information in the 'Spies for Peace' document. We were assured that 'vigorous steps are being taken'.

During that April also the Enaharo case was brought up in the House of Commons. The unfortunate Chief Enaharo, finally deported back to Nigeria to face trial for treason because of being denied asylum in this country owing to having the misfortune of being a Commonwealth citizen, plays no part in this story, except that the distressing muddle over his case emphasised the failure of judgment that was now spreading like a creeping infection along the Front Government Bench, leaving out no one, not even the most habitually level-headed member of the Government. Indeed, for this last reason, the Enaharo case was the most alarming incident of all to the close observer of the parliamentary scene.

Finally, Dr. Stephen Ward did not disappear. As the

Denning Report reveals, whether it was from loss of nerve when he knew that on the Home Secretary's instructions the police were investigating his activities, or whether from some pre-planned nefarious design, he started to talk—or, at least, write—like a babbling brook. Eventually, round about 20th May, a series of letters reached such people as the Home Secretary, Sir Wavell Wakefield (the Conservative M.P. for the Marylebone Division), Mr. Harold Wilson (then Leader of the Opposition). All these letters contained the shattering allegation, supported by evidence, that Profumo had, despite his denial, slept with Christine Keeler. Mr. Harold Wilson passed this on to the Prime Minister. Labour Members were starting to table Questions and Profumo had various background interviews with the Chief Whip and the Prime Minister's Private Secretary.

In due course, he saw both these gentlemen on Tuesday, 4th June, and finally in almost George Washington fashion, he declared 'I have to tell you that I did sleep with Miss Keeler'.

As Lord Denning tersely puts it, 'It was plain, of course, that he could not remain a Member of the administration.' Lord Denning vouchsafes no explanation as to whether this was because Profumo lay or because he lied.

*   *   *   *   *

It was indicative of the 'mixed-up kid' state of the Macmillan Government that it should have mattered so much that Jack Profumo had slept with Christine Keeler. (This will probably remain a mystery to our French friends for all eternity.)

However, the emphasis on the sex angle in Profumo's statement in the House of Commons on 22nd March had created a Micawberish situation. Profumo had already admitted his questionable associations and that, as I personally had felt at the time, was surely good enough—or bad enough, if it is put the other way round. But now, owing to the grave mismanagement of this occasion, the fate of the nation was balanced on this ridiculous hair's breadth. If the Minister's relationship with Christine Keeler was virtuous, confidence in the Government would remain: if on the other hand it was not, the Government would go down to ruin and destruction. It was a strange absurdity that the fate of the nation's traditional Establishment should depend on just this—a few hours spent, or not spent, by a single individual in bed.

But in existing circumstances it did matter. As the news of the Profumo confession and resignation came out, a wave of outraged feeling swept the country against his using the House of Commons despatch box for an untrue statement, together with a sense of bewilderment at the contrast between the proud dignity of the façade of Conservatism and the squalid actualities of the Ward-Keeler associations. With the 'image' of the austere Establishment dragged in the mire, there was the deep consciousness that something basic and fundamental had happened: and that, as Mr. Hugh Massingham had predicted, things would never be the same again. For at least three or four days, Mr. Harold Macmillan had 'never had it so bad'. For public discussion quickly centred on a single point. The Prime Minister had sanctioned the original Profumo statement in the House with his presence and his active approval. His was the ultimate responsibility. Should he go or should he stay? If he was to go, when?

To my own generation it was almost a *déja vu* situation. Just as the First World War had been followed twenty years later by the Second World War: so now twenty years later again, we were at a Dunkirk of the Cold War—with the sick Harold Macmillan, a shadow of his one-time self, succeeding to the role of the sick Neville Chamberlain.*

It was a time of signs and portents—sometimes, it seemed, straight from the pages of Shakespeare—only to be explained by the manifestation of higher forces into our lowly sphere of human life at a time of major cataclysm. The present cataclysm being the end of the many hundreds of years' rule of the Old Establishment.

For there was no Churchill this time, either to give a lead

---

* Neville Chamberlain died of intestinal cancer in November 1940. This slow-growing disease must have been sapping his strength during his Premiership in the early days of the War throughout 1939 and early 1940.

to patriotic feeling, or to save the Old Establishment. Luck, as I have said, had run right out. Even the ability to produce a leader as at the time of Dunkirk had deserted them. The Old Establishment had nothing left.

★   ★   ★   ★   ★

Once again, coincidence started to feature in my life. But whereas in previous instances in my story, such coincidences had been peculiar to me alone, now in several instances they related to wider contexts, being moreover no mere matters of imagination.

Mr. John Profumo's confession on 4th June occurred at the beginning of the short Whitsun recess. This day was Betty's fortieth birthday and we had arranged a motoring tour northwards in celebration of this event. Likewise, the long-appointed day for a meeting with my Officers in Carlisle had come due.

It will be recollected from my first chapter that I had written to the Chairman of the Carlisle Conservative Association immediately after the Profumo statement in the House in March saying that I did not want to bother him urgently, but that I would like to discuss my position with him in due course. The weeks and months had passed by, the Council Elections in May (during which the majority of the Conservative Association Executive had been more involved in their own Council affairs than in any business of mine) had come and gone, and finally it was fixed as Thursday, 6th June, before, free of their own preoccupations, they were able to listen to what I had to say. We were then due—overdue even—for a further one of the series of get-togethers which, since the grave misunderstandings of the previous year, had been a feature of an attempt to establish better relationships between my officers and myself.

So it was that, with the morning paper containing the 'release' of the Profumo confession in my hand, Betty and I, newly arrived in Carlisle, stepped across from 'The Crown and Mitre', where we were staying, to the late tea-party at 'The

Silver Grill' round which my formidable friends were gathered.

On this occasion even the Officers of my Association could not help themselves but agree with me. This was the moment of truth: the moment when, even to them, black was black and white was white, the moment before the correct line of Party 'rationalisation' had been inculcated into them and they were helpless in the face of the facts.

About Macmillan, about Profumo, they agreed with me all along the line. But they had their reservations. This was not —definitely not—a matter for public comment! No! No! No!

But what was the purpose in keeping silent at a time when the nation was in danger? This was the conflict of thought that haunted me first throughout the following week-end, which we spent in the less restrictive atmosphere of the Annual Booksellers' Conference at Harrogate, then in the course of our drive back to London.

As Monday moved along to Tuesday during the following week, and Tuesday to Wednesday, a parodoxical state of affairs arose throughout the country. Everyone, yes everyone, was talking privately about Macmillan and Profumo, with hubbubs of conversation in every bar and social gathering: while, on the other hand, the entire world of public life, this being still the time of the parliamentary recess, was maintaining a stunned and apprehensive silence. Nobody was saying a single word. In such circumstances, I felt that this was my appointment with destiny. More and more, I had the compulsion to speak out, even if only to express the sense of desperation felt by so many seriously thinking people. I had nothing to gain by speaking—indeed I was quite certain to incur the odium of the Officers of my Association once again. On the other hand 'The Establishment' had manoeuvred me into the position in which I had nothing to lose either. For what 'sanction' did even the mighty Officers of the Carlisle Conservative Association have, when I was so deprived of interest that I was ready to abandon Parliament, anyway?

Edward Martell was the deciding factor.

Busy as ever stepping into breaches, Edward phoned me excitedly on Wednesday morning with the results of the

referendum which his paper, *The New Daily*, had already been
conducting amongst its readership. Should Macmillan stay or
should he go? Should he go before the Debate which had
now been announced for the opening of the summer session
the following Monday, 17th June? Edward's poll was to be
announced the following morning and when it appeared it
was of a decisive character:

> Mr. Macmillan should resign from the
> Premiership before next Monday's Debate   1423
> Mr. Macmillan should not resign..   ..   342

It was time for action, for someone to give a lead. There
was no valid reason why I should not do so.

The die was finally cast that same evening in Edward's
slightly dingy office at Tileyard House, Islington. The statement which I issued was brief and to the point:

> 'No one can fail to sympathise with the Prime Minister
> in his present position. The fact remains, however, that it is
> becoming clearer day by day that, if the Party is to survive
> at the General Election, he should resign, so that we can
> rally round a fresh leader for Monday's debate.'

'Dr. Johnson echoes the opinion of many backbenchers,'
said 'Brutus' of *The New Daily*, the following morning—and
you can, of course, guess at the identity of 'Brutus'—'But
whether any of them will have the courage to say so publicly
is another matter. I know three who are endeavouring to
screw themselves up to the point of ranging themselves beside
Dr. Johnson. But I doubt if they'll make it. Most Conservative
backbenchers are frightened men. Frightened of upsetting the
Whips. Frightened of upsetting their constituency Chairmen.
Some of them frightened of losing their jobs, and the income
that goes with them.'

'Though Conservative discontent is plain enough, its extent
and intensity are still hard to assess while the House is not
sitting,' said Edward Greenfield of *The Guardian* more cautiously,

'Dr. Donald Johnson, the Member for Carlisle, yesterday won the distinction of being the first Conservative in the present crisis to call for the Prime Minister's resignation . . . one of his (the Prime Minister's) great sources of strength all along has been that there is no one successor of whom the whole party would be agreed.'

I was not conscious of any particular distinction during the following four days that intervened between my statement and Monday's debate, though certainly it was Olympian in its way to be able to sit at home in one's armchair, pick up the phone to the Press Association and the Exchange Telegraph, and issue statements which one knew would be boomed across all the channels of communication to emerge shortly on TV News, in the morning papers, and so on.

However it was as if destiny was declaring itself in spite of me, and my sub-conscious mind was taking over. These coincidences to which I have already referred could well be identified with what that famous psychiatrist, the late Professor Jung, termed in his own phraseology 'events of non-causal synchonicity which are connected with the archetypes'. There would be small personal coincidences that coincided with coincidences in a larger and wider sphere. I would be reading the paper in the train on the way home to Sutton: I would be looking at the financial page and a note about 'Hackbridge Holdings', then I would look out of the window as we were stopped at a station and find that this was Hackbridge Station —that sort of thing. Then, as the day of Monday's important debate approached, the customary document of the Three-Line Whip arrived through the post with the familiar signature of Martin Redmayne. By the next post there came a second missive—the 'anti-Whip', as it were—it was also signed 'Martin'—it was from Martin Lindsay'* complimenting me on my statement and asking me to abstain at the debate. The handwriting of the two Martins was almost identical.

Whether it was the operation of Professor Jung's archetypes or not, I found myself moving about in a kind of trance— keeping appointments in the nick of time, catching my

* Sir Martin Lindsay, Conservative M.P. for Solihull, 1945–64.

suburban trains with moments to spare, as if carried forward on the wave of time, like an automaton.

For I was not left peacefully in my armchair at home for long. Apart from newsmen and, of course, Edward Martell phoning me with almost a minute by minute commentary on his campaign, I suddenly became a magnet for old acquaintances whom I had not seen for long enough, but who now became possessed with a compulsive urge to see me to tell me some worry of their own, each of which fitted curiously enough into the jigsaw puzzle of my own imaginings about the far-flung schemes of World Communism.

Amongst other messages which I receive was one to ring Mr. Horobin at Holborn 7690 and in no time at all, it seemed, I was in the ITN studios in Television House, Kingsway, chatting it up with the TV boys, preparatory to being interviewed by John Whale on the national network. ITN had already given prominence to my statement, even going to the trouble of finding a reasonably presentable photograph of me in the brief time between the 6 p.m. and the 9 p.m. news.

There was no doubt that the TV boys were with me.

'You're on a good thing,' they assured me. 'Don't all you people realise that everyone has been laughing at your Prime Minister for months?'

It was cheering to find that I had support. But it was clear —unfortunately only at a later date—that they had underestimated the power of their own medium.

In the meantime I once again got myself involved in argument. My detractors at the BBC were starting to undermine me and within forty-eight hours I had to issue a second statement in the following terms:

'It was implied on BBC television last night that I do not count for very much in Party affairs. I do, however, count to some extent owing to the fact that I hold a marginal seat which I cannot possibly fight at the General Election as long as Mr. Macmillan is Prime Minister. I say this now in the interests of the Party.

'Other commentators seem to me to have missed the

point in the Profumo affair. It is conspicuously true that sex and politics do not mix and, in this instance, Mr. Profumo's greatest error was, in fact, to mix them by his unnecessarily long, and equally untrue, statement in the House of Commons, which was unfortunately supported by the Prime Minister through his presence on the Front Bench.

'It was the element of exhibitionism in this episode that has unfortunately brought both Prime Minister and Party into widespread ridicule which it is impossible for any person of professional standing to answer on a public platform.'

This certainly obtained further publicity for my views. But I had allowed myself to be trapped into mortal sin! To threaten resignation from a marginal constituency in such an open fashion as this is the most heinous crime of all in the closely knit world of the Party. Probably, could one investigate completely the causes of my ruin, my fate was sealed from that moment.

None the less, I made my point. I could only guess at the time the jokes that might be circulating round the pubs. This is one.

Question: What does Christine Keeler like best?

Answer: A bedtime Tory.

It only remains to say that this one was told to me in Carlisle (after a few drinks) by one of those men who was to oppose me most bitterly.

As Monday's debate approached, the nation was, as I have said, in a turmoil of speculation with its eyes and ears, in the shape of the political correspondents, endeavouring to estimate how this M.P. would vote or whether that M.P. would abstain: and how secure was the Prime Minister with his majority. Above all, how many abstentions of Tory M.P.s could he afford to have before being forced to resign?

Even the resignation bug was spreading and, by the end of the week, such place as I held in the nation's eye was usurped by that chronic resigner, Mr. Enoch Powell. 'Insistent on the moral issue,' Enoch Powell kept everybody guessing for a day or more before, on this occasion, deciding to stay.

At the time of the announcement of the Profumo confession on the previous Thursday, Mr. Harold Macmillan himself had been playing golf at Gleneagles and, imperturbable as ever, he had not returned to London until the Sunday morning, still making no comment. Now he too was caught up in the excitement to the extent that on Wednesday he was reported as being so preoccupied that he omitted to remove his hat for the opening bars of the National Anthem when meeting the President of India at Victoria Station.

That this was a week of nervous tension for others beside myself was all too obvious. If the Prime Minister was slightly absent-minded, the Government appeared more and more 'bonkers' as the days passed. Enoch Powell's dash to Wolverhampton to contemplate his non-resignation was starred as if it were Dick Turpin's ride to York; the emotional intensity of Lord Hailsham's Thursday's TV appearance was such that one commentator alleged that his head appeared to change shape as he spoke.

How would the dispersed and secretive Tory M.P.s vote when they reassembled for the 'Confidence' debate on Monday? With the reported widespread doubtings amongst Tory backbenchers, were there any others, besides myself, who would abstain from supporting the Prime Minister? If so, how many? The political correspondents sought them here and sought them there, but without obtaining satisfactory answers. By the end of the week the position had crystallised to a consensus that the number of abstentions from the Party vote at the end of the debate would be the factor that would decide the Prime Minister's fate. (Just as, of course, it decided the fate of Neville Chamberlain in 1940—though in those days there were also M.P.s who were so committed as to vote against their own Party.) However, in the present instance, it was decided that, if there were forty abstentions the Prime Minister would have to go: if there were thirty, he might just survive: if there were only twenty, he could stay on. The course was marked out just as clearly as that: and the uncertainty of the prospect was sending the pundits of the Party completely frantic.

Once again the situation was such that any step taken could only lead deeper into the mire. This did not prevent the ebullient Lord Hailsham from rushing forward to take such a step. The first thing, so it was evidently considered in high quarters, was to allay public anxiety that the Three-Line Whip now being sent out to Tory Members was in any way dragooning unwilling Members of Parliament to vote against their consciences on a moral issue. I had made a rider to my own statement which I have just quoted to the effect that I did not recognise the moral authority of this particular Whip.

This Whip, which was now going out and on which the fate of both Prime Minister and Party depended, was (so Lord Hailsham assured his listeners on TV) no compulsion to vote at all. It was 'merely' (and I think that was the word he used) a 'summons to attend' in order 'to listen to the arguments'.

Hailsham's humbug about the 'summons to attend' was really too much for me. It was meant to be reassuring, but on me it had the opposite effect. I was quite satisfied as to my familiarity with the cogent arguments. I was past the point of no return and I had only one problem to solve: how to spend my day? Enough was enough and I wanted to be away from it all. One would be hunted down with futile argument even in the Interview Rooms passage: my mind flew back to my only place of refuge in the days when I was a doctor in general practice—the golf course. I would go and play golf.

It somehow got around that it was my intention to play golf. It was during the course of Friday afternoon that I ran into Douglas Clark, then editor of 'Cross Bencher' column in the *Sunday Express*, in New Palace Yard.

'Do keep this one for me!' said Douglas Clark.

'All right', I agreed.

Douglas Clark did the story justice. For this is what appeared in 'Cross Bencher' in Sunday's issue:

'After tomorrow's high drama in the Commons, what are Mr. Harold Macmillan's intentions?

'Assuming he gets an adequate vote of confidence, will he stay on to lead the Tory Party through the next General Election?

'All the speculation in political circles says he will not.

'Into the ear of every Tory M.P. this guidance about the Premier's plans is being whispered.

'He will remain till the excitement over the Profumo affair has died down.

'Then—probably late next month—he will take his earldom.

'And the Party will march to its autumn conference at Blackpool under the revivalist inspiration of a new chief.

'Whence comes this guidance?

'From very high Party quarters indeed.

'And, of course, it is likely to assist Mr. Macmillan in the Profumo debate.

'For it will disarm Tory M.P.s who are torn between uneasiness over his leadership and fear that by failing to vote for him they might bring down the whole Government.

'After all, if the Premier is going anyway in a few weeks time, why rock the boat to-morrow?

ONE QUERY

'But there is just one query which will nag at the minds of Mr. Macmillan's back-bench critics as they consider how to vote to-morrow night.

'When the dust has settled on the Profumo affair might he not decide to remain after all?

OFF TO THE SEA

'Of course, for certain Tories, to-morrow's division presents no problem at all.

'In no circumstances would they vote for the Government.

'And they may even absent themselves from the debate altogether.

'How, for instance, does Dr. Donald McIntosh Johnson, Carlisle's burly rebel M.P., plan to spend the day?

'He tells me: "If the weather is fine, I'm off to Littlestone-on-Sea. Splendid golf course there."

'What you might call the Gleneagles Touch.'

Douglas Clark's prediction made on my behalf was correct. When Parliament reassembled at 2.30 p.m. on Monday most other colleagues were there, listening or otherwise to the persuasions of the Whips and, doubtless also to the speeches in the Debating Chamber: but, in company with Betty—and the inevitable Press photographer—I was on the first tee at Littlestone.

A fine day and a 'first half' score of 47 made the afternoon a worthwhile excursion for an indifferent golfer. At the far end of the course, which runs along the sea coast, I found waiting for me on the 11th tee two further representatives of the Press observer squad, who accompanied me back on a less successful second half.

On our way home in the car Betty drew my attention to the fact that, in the course of my friendly conversation with them, I had 'unwound' in somewhat indiscreet fashion. It was only at a very much later date that I discovered that these particular 'famous last words' were repeated in the northern editions of the *Daily Express* the following morning.

However, in addition to the photographers and the reporters, we must undoubtedly have had company of which we were not at first aware on this quiet, relaxed game of golf. Surely the 'gremlin' of Professor Jung's 'non-causal synchronicity'? We were enjoying our club house tea together after the round when Betty pointed to the table mats on which our tea cups rested—sure enough, they were embellished with pictures of *The Laughing Cavalier*—Betty's old friend, whom she had seen winking at her from the walls of the bedroom at the Marlborough Arms Hotel, Woodstock, during our incident in October 1950. (One of these mats, kindly signed by the Club Secretary on the spot and traded in return for a presentation copy of *Bars and Barricades* still decorates the shelf of our lounge at home.) In addition to this we had been fortunate enough to find a new ball in the long grass at the 18th hole: it was a 'Warwick'. There was nothing unusual about this, until it suddenly came to us that this was another coincidence with our Woodstock episode, inasmuch as that it was at that time that we had discovered that the geneological tree of Betty's family, the Plaisteds, led back to John du Plessis, 9th Earl of Warwick in the thirteenth century. Destiny itself, so it seemed, what'er befall, was with us in our lonely venture.

The debate at Westminster was, of course, a historic one. Nigel Birch's quotation from Robert Browning's 'The Lost Leader'—'Never glad, confident morning again'—will be remembered when all else, including even my own game of golf, will be forgotten. Lord Lambton made a notable protest, which will be seen a little later on to endorse the arguments of this book.

But, reduced to dumb crambo, as I was in my role as a Member of Parliament, I had at least put up a show. REBEL NUMBER SHAKES WHIPS: 27 TORIES ABSTAIN declared the headline on the following morning's *Daily Express* front page. In the middle of the account of the debate beneath this was a horizontal strip-picture of myself swinging a golf club on the first tee at Littlestone.

69 majority sets off uproar declares the sub-headline still in bold type above a picture of a seedy-looking Harold Macmillan.

Indeed, following this debate there ensued no end of speculation. Nobody knew what would happen, but all sensed that the Prime Ministership of Mr. Harold Macmillan, the future of the Tory Party, and much else besides, were in the melting pot. It needed, however, the penetrating mind of Henry Kerby to point out the sexual connotation of the exotic number, 69. I am not sure what the late Professor Jung would have made of this one.

CHAPTER TWELVE

THE GREAT SICKNESS OF THE CONSERVATIVE PARTY

THE PRIME MINISTER was saved. Mr. Harold Macmillan had just 'touched down'. At the head of the *Daily Express* front page to which I have already referred, there he was, in cartoon by Cummings, the exhausted runner who had just made the winning post by flinging himself out at full length.

It had been a narrow victory, but a victory just the same.

His explanation was that he had been deceived. Nobody had told him. Lord Normanbrook, then Secretary to the Cabinet, had warned Mr. Profumo about his association with Dr. Stephen Ward in August 1961, but had not told the Prime Minister. The Security Services had not passed on to him the reports that Miss Christine Keeler had been asked to get 'atomic information' from Mr. John Profumo.

During the debate this explanation had not impressed his listeners on the back benches. The real issue was, of course, 'the Party'. The 1922 Committee of backbenchers had met prior to the debate. For reasons that I have explained, my authority must be based on contemporary reports. Clive Irving in his *Scandal '63** alleges that 'the impression was given that, if the Party that night supported Mr. Macmillan at the Division, they could tacitly assume that he would not remain in office for very much longer'.

My personal information gives me no occasion to disagree with this statement. More than one of my colleagues voted for Prime Minister and Party for no other reason that that they

* *Scandal '63*, by Clive Irving (Heinemann and Co., 1964).

received an authoritative assurance of this nature. Though, of course, they should have known better in the light of past experience.

On the morning after the debate it was widely assumed, therefore, that this bargain would be honoured and that the Prime Minister would soon go. 'Premier likely to resign soon,' was the headline in the *Daily Telegraph*: 'Mac: the End,' said the *Daily Mail* briefly.

The Party was saved; the Prime Minister was going. Everyone felt reasonably satisfied with the sole possible exception of Mr. Harold Macmillan himself.

During the days succeeding the Profumo debate my customary assiduous attendance at Westminster still lapsed. It was the week of the Annual Conference of the Union of Post Office Workers: for this week my 'pair', Bill Williams, transferred his conscientious attendances to Brighton, Margate, Bournemouth or wherever other delectable resort this happened to be. Over the years I had come to look on this week when I had a pair, not only from 9 p.m. onwards, but for the whole day, as an annual mid-term holiday. At the present juncture I was not sorry to have the opportunity of allowing any untoward impressions created by the publicity surrounding my game of golf to simmer down for a day or two before I reappeared. Though I discovered later that I need not have been quite so squeamish as far as Westminster was concerned.

It was essential, however, for me to visit Carlisle.

Hitherto, throughout the years, my personal popularity among the electors of Carlisle had been the least of my worries. My Association Officers might protest, but even at times of greatest tension, I was confident that my image as an active Member and my general attentiveness to my constituents' needs would pull me through—as it had until now. Whate'er befall, I could count on a smiling welcome when I emerged from the Citadel Station and walked out past the Courts along to the central promenade of English Street.

As I travelled up on the Wednesday two days after the Profumo debate (and my own game of golf), I had no other thought but that I would retain the confidence of 'the man in the street' in Carlisle in my protest. A certain allegiance to the old-fashioned virtues which characterised the people in this isolated place would (I told myself) lead them to rally round me in the censorious attitude which I had taken.

It was only when I arrived in Carlisle and made my customary tour of the main streets that I realised how mistaken I had been. Gone were the smiles and the welcoming greetings. The people of Carlisle were in censorious mood, but I had only to look around me to perceive that it was neither Mr. Harold Macmillan, nor even Mr. John Profumo, who were the objects of their disapproval—it was I myself.

I did not have 'the Gleneagles touch' after all! I lacked the knack. It was soon apparent that my well-publicised game of golf had been too much for them. Suddenly, too, I was aware that Carlisle had changed, even during the short time I had known it.

'You've been the best Member we've ever had and now you go and play golf and spoil it all,' lamented my old friend, Harold Robinson, who had been Chairman of the Denton Holme Conservative Working Men's Club over the years.

Harold was quite right. I was never to live down my game of golf.

When, later on the afternoon of which I write, I got amongst the loyal Conservatives, it was worse still. Those who had never previously shown the least interest in my strivings in Parliament, were now outraged that I had not 'represented' them on so important an occasion—though how I could have represented them other than by sitting silently about the place at Westminster, they had no knowledge. Others, equally ignorant, asked me why, if I wanted to protest, I had not gone to the debate and spoken up like Nigel Birch. It was virtually waste of time to explain to such people that Nigel Birch, being a Privy Councillor, had the prerogative of being called on to speak, while, judging by all previous form, I could have sat in the Debating Chamber, silent and frustrated until Doomsday, without having the opportunity to say a word.

It was useless to say anything then. I can only hope that, by the time many of them come to read these words, they will have found a better understanding, gained, alas, by hard experience in the meantime.

Somewhat bewildered at the time, I was soon to appreciate that I had crashed head on into the wave of sentimental sympathy which, quite unintelligibly, had started to sweep the country in favour of the Prime Minister, the innocent man, the victim of those who had let him down by not telling him anything, and of those others who were now 'betraying' him by denying him their support in his difficulties.

As I sat on the platform at the Denton Holme Working Men's Conservative Club that evening on the occasion of the Annual General Meeting, I was uncomfortably aware of the resentment directed at me from the tensely watching audience. In this place, where over the years I had been welcomed so cordially, it now looked as if I was in for a pretty bad time. It was fortunate that, during the course of the business proceedings, a bitter quarrel sprang up over the price of beer—thus relieving the thundery atmosphere of the meeting—so that I was able to get away with an evasive statement to the effect that I would explain myself in due course.

The only thing, I felt, was to play for time and wait for all this to blow over.

I was confident that, as far as Mr. Macmillan was concerned, time would be on my side. So it was. But unfortunately there was not quite enough of it. In the meantime, I managed to obtain my Association Officers' agreement to a three-months stand-still until it could be ascertained whether Mr. Macmillan was staying or going—and, of course, when.

That was the question that overhung all else in politics during the remainder of those summer months.

*   *   *   *   *

It was the fashion then, and still to some extent is now, to condemn those who had the temerity to declare, as I did, that it was necessary for Mr. Harold Macmillan to resign before that crucial Monday's debate, if the Conservative Party was to be saved.

But who now can say that we were wrong?

It would have been bad to have a Prime Minister retire on account of a scandal with such squalid overtones. It would not, however, have been as bad as what took place. For though the Party still lives as a shell of its former self, it was those summer months of 1963 which saw the destruction of its deepest faiths as a democratic Party. Signs and portents had abounded during the critical days preceding the debate, but now came the doom which these had foreshadowed in the shape of the clear demonstration of the utter impotence of the back-bench M.P. The time had come when the Tory Party ceased to embody British representative democracy.

For, despite such assurances as may have been given about Mr. Harold Macmillan's impending resignation in order to persuade Tory M.P.s to vote on the night of Monday, 17th June, the days passed by and action failed to develop. Those who had expected something further from the meeting of the 1922 Committee on the Thursday, three days later, were disappointed when they found the discussion side-tracked by a lengthy dissertation by Sir Derek Walker-Smith. Soon, a week had passed and, despite the dire newspaper headlines on the day following the debate, Mr. Macmillan was still there, apparently imperturbable as ever.

Indeed, as the wave of sympathy which I had met in Carlisle manifested itself throughout the country, there appeared correspondingly less and less hurry on the part of Mr. Macmillan to retire.

Within the fortnight, on Friday, 28th June, Mr. Harold Macmillan made his position plain in an interview at Wolverhampton.

'I have received messages of encouragement from every part and every section of the British people on a scale which I have never known.

'All being well,' he said, 'if I keep my health and strength, I hope to lead the Party into the election . . . of course, I must have the support of the Party and I think I have it.'

The Government had a great deal of work to do, he added.

Clive Irving in *Scandal '63* uses words of masterly understatement. Conservative M.P.s who, feeling themselves deceived, were 'by this time after his blood', had been 'brilliantly outmanoeuvred'.

Lord Lambton put the position clearly in his analysis in the *Evening Standard* of 1st July:

> 'What this means, in effect, is that Mr. Macmillan has decided that the loyalty which the parliamentary party gave him all through last year . . . now counts for nothing and that he denies it any right in choosing who is to be its leader.
>
> 'Furthermore, to gain his end, he is prepared to get an unelected chairman of the party in the person of Lord Poole to tour the country telling M.P.s that they have no right to speak out, and behind the scenes putting pressure upon constituency leaders to call their Members to heel.
>
> 'In fact, the crisis has now become constitutional, for what Mr. Macmillan is attempting to establish is an auto-cracy with Members of Parliament under the control of the Central Office machine.'

This was correct. The crisis in Conservative affairs had escalated far beyond the bed of Miss Christine Keeler. This mischievous young lady had triggered off a train of events which was now involving a crisis of democracy. The ubiquitous Lord Poole, former Conservative M.P. for Oswestry and now Joint Chairman of the Conservative Party, Director of White-hall Securities—and who, moving about the globe, could have failed to run into the trail of Lord Poole in his business capacity during those years?—had been as ubiquitous as ever, Newcastle, Birmingham, Manchester, the message had been the same to Conservative officials in the Provinces.

'Mr. Macmillan has the right, and he has the duty, to make his own decision in his own way. Moreover he is entitled to make it calmly and unhurriedly. We can be sure that in his final judgment he will be governed by one thing only: the national interests.'

As a businessman, Lord Poole's enviable reputation has been to see to the heart of a problem; and this time both the problem and its situation were simple, in just the manner that Lambton had explained. M.P.s could be sorted out without difficulty once their Associations were lined up against them.

*   *   *   *   *

The position of Mr. Harold Macmillan was now almost unique in the history of British politics.

It was a year since his *putsch* of July 1962 since when he had stood above the political scene like the Monarch of the Glen, proud, aloof—and alone.

First there had gone the senior members of his Cabinet. Kilmuir, Eccles, Hill, Lloyd, Watkinson and others— eliminated overnight in Stalinesque fashion, leaving but a rump of senior Tory survivors, none of whom, in the light of their colleagues' fate, could have ventured to differ greatly at any time from their chief.

Now, in July 1963, back-bench M.P.s had been 'out-manoeuvred' and were being treated with contempt.

It seemed as if, with the support of Lord Poole and the Conservative organisation throughout the country, combined with an occasional TV appearance, Mr. Harold Macmillan could rule in autocratic fashion for as long as he liked. Members of Parliament, apart from providing regimented votes in the Lobby, were redundant operators.

There was but one flaw on this noble picture. It was clear that the Monarch of the Glen was tottering on his feet, his head was dropping, his eye was glazing over. Mr. Harold Macmillan was not well.

*   *   *   *   *

The Great Sickness of the Conservative Party which now ensued will inevitably be eclipsed as a feature of historical interest by the Great Sickness of Mr. Harold Macmillan, and it is well therefore that in my story this latter should be given precedence.

Following the operation on his enlarged prostate gland and

its safe removal in October of that year, all his personal well-wishers have been pleased to learn of his recovery in health.

In view of the political manifestations in 1963 retrospective speculation is naturally rife as to the effect of Mr. Macmillan's complaint both on his general health and his pattern of behaviour in the months that preceded the culminating moment when he decided on operative cure in October.

It is common medical knowledge that neglect of an enlarged prostate gland causes retention of the urine, back-pressure on the kidneys and an accumulation in the blood of the poison, urea, with its consequent effect upon the human system, both physical and nervous. Strange and unusual alterations of human behaviour are associated with a high blood urea: above all, a lassitude and a remoteness such as Mr. Harold Macmillan exhibited during that crucial time.

The measurement of Mr. Harold Macmillan's blood urea during these vital months is one of the best kept medical secrets of the present day. While this is understandable, it can only be hoped that, for the benefit of historians of the future, it will one day be revealed. For it will surely occupy the same importance in the minds of students of the medical history of the present day, as does the hemiplegia of President Wilson, the paralysis of Roosevelt, the paranoia of Stalin and the illnesses of other prominent statesmen.

In the meantime I can only hope that my observations as an onlooker with some years experience of medical diagnosis will be of assistance to them.

I have been reasonably free throughout this book with my comments on Mr. Harold Macmillan, but there is no sign whatsoever that his political behaviour, much as it can be criticised, transgressed normal bounds, until we come to 13th July 1962, and the instant dismissal of the seven Cabinet Ministers, friends and colleagues of a lifetime, carried out, so it has been said, at the greatest personal distress of the Prime Minister himself. The result of the North-East Leicester by-election on the previous day had been disastrous for the Conservatives. However, one of the victims, the Earl of Kilmuir, 'sacked' after he had only a fortnight previously been refused permission to go abroad in that same autumn, remarks that 'It astonished me that a man who had kept his head under the most severe stresses and strains should lose both nerve and judgment in this way.'* Lord Hill also criticises the way things were done: in a hurry.** (As if the departing men 'had been caught with their hands in the till', as one commentator put it.)

There is no better illustration of the regimental nature of the Conservative Party than the fact that all these men went without comment, without protest, without any form of discussion or speculation. But was there a common denominator in these 'sackings'? The suggestion has been bruited in more disrespectful circles that the evicted members of the Cabinet were merely a lot of non-U middle-aged people cluttering up the place and barring the way to the young, the progressive and the well-born, whom we have met previously in this story and this is probably the truth. The names of those 'sacked'—Lloyd, Hill, Maclay, Watkinson, Eccles, Kilmuir, Mills—would suggest that the Prime Minister had done a hurried human acrostic in which he decided to rid himself of all non-Etonians over the age of forty-five. Though this action was in harmony with Mr. Harold Macmillan's trend of thought, it was certainly a bizarre extension of it. The only parallel one can think of is the alleged edict of the first Lord Northcliffe to sack all red-headed men working on the *Daily Mail*.

(Perhaps too these self-made men may have been too persistent as questioners on delicate issues? If so, the Prime Minister failed to do a thorough job. For it was the man he overlooked, Henry Brooke, who, as the Denning Report reveals, was responsible for his ultimate downfall on account of the instructions which the latter as Home Secretary gave to the police to investigate the doings of Stephen Ward at a critical moment of the Profumo affair.)

It was certainly an unforgettable moment, when, sitting as an observer in the Debating Chamber of the House of

* *Political Adventure*, p. 323.
** *Both Sides of the Hill*, by Lord Hill of Luton (Heinemann and Co., 1964).

Commons during the Censure Debate on the Dissolution of Parliament on 20th July 1962, one saw the drawn and anxious-looking Prime Minister, explaining his 'sackings', pointing to a robust-looking Selwyn Lloyd on the back benches as an example of a tired man, best relieved of his duties so that he could take a rest. 'I must say that the former Chancellor of the Exchequer looks far more ruddy and healthy and wide-awake than any of these new Ministers' remarked Mr. Hugh Gaitskell during the debate—and he was quite right.

This, however, is merely speculation.

But, coming to the spring and summer of 1963, there could no longer be any doubt that Mr. Harold Macmillan was ill. Discomforting stories were circulating of interviews in which he had scarcely said anything at all relevant to the matter in hand, of top doctors expressing alarm at his state of health when in July he appeared as Guest of Honour at the Dinner of the British Medical Association Annual Conference at Oxford. One's mind inevitably flew back to make comparison with the disintegrating Mr. Ramsay Macdonald of thirty years previously.

The endemic problem of political party democracy once again ensued—the rally round the failing leader, whose public image must be shielded from the truth. Once Mr. Harold Macmillan had made it quite clear in his announcement on 1st July that he intended to stay and it was equally clear that there were no rivals, the rally was an impressive one. In the light of my own commitment, it was with some sense of dismay that I watched while, through one alchemy or the other, all those organs of opinion, which had featured me so generously as a critic, were now rooting hard for Mr. Harold Macmillan, while his critics were given scant grace. This process was eventually highlighted by the threatened resignation of Mr. John Junor from the *Sunday Express*—a courageous gesture fortunately unconsummated owing to the retirement of Mr. Macmillan in time to save this particular situation. Mr. Junor had more generous-minded employers than I did.

Meanwhile, those who had been elected to be watchdogs of the public interest and who had the scene in high quarters under the closest scrutiny were thrust aside. It was an agonising time for Conservative back-bench Members of Parliament, crushed into political impotence between a Prime Minister with a predeliction for instant dismissal, Joint Party Chairmen, such as Lord Poole and Iain Macleod, zealous in his support, and the unreasoning sentimentality of members of Constituency Associations.

Little wonder that, on occasions, there were breakdowns of morale. The *Daily Telegraph* account of the 1922 Committee meeting on 28th June mentions that 'a gorgeous row turned into a gale of laughter' following a well-intentioned speech by Sir Cyril Osborne, that 'the meeting exploded with laughter' at a simple interchange between Major Morrison, the Chairman, and Viscount Lambton; it refers to reports of the 'schoolboyish level of discussion' in the course of which Lord Poole was accused of being 'altogether too dictatorial'.

Accounts of an unofficial kind emanating from a secret Party meeting can often fairly be accused of being garbled. But this one was not. I was present myself at this meeting and the newspaper report only erred in understatement. I had difficulty joining in the laughter: indeed, as I sat at the back of the room, a silent spectator of the current proceedings of this normally proud and dignified, rather starchy assembly, I was overcome with a feeling of alarm such as I have seldom experienced.

It was credibly reported that as many as eighty back-benchers were leagued together to remove Mr. Harold Macmillan from the leadership (this was quite true—I was personally aware of most of their names and identities) but it was impossible for any member of the Press to discover either who these people were or indeed the identity of anyone who would publicly associate himself with such a movement. The Press tended to turn this situation much to derision: but in the light of my own subsequent experience, the reticence of my colleagues is understandable.

For myself, however, I had burnt my boats irrevocably on the day of the Profumo debate. My feelings of alarm about the national situation, moreover, did not abate.

Evidence of further security failures was still emerging when, on 1st July, Edward Heath, as spokesman for the Foreign Office, was having to admit the truth about the Philby story—namely that, despite the Government denials at the time, Mr. Marcus Lipton (Labour M.P. for Brixton) had been right in his allegations in the House some years previously that Philby had been 'the third man' in the Burgess and Maclean case.

I can scarcely be blamed if in my imagination I wandered back to the warnings from my Woodstock episode. Here were the *élite* of the country publicly destroying themselves through exhibitions of confusion and absurd behaviour! What was the explanation?

I kept my more fanciful hypotheses to myself and perhaps this was just as well. As I left home one morning activity at the manhole outside on the pavement aroused my curiosity:

'Just improving your telephone service, sir', volunteered one of the human beavers at work.

In any case, at the head of affairs there was still Mr. Harold Macmillan, who had made it clear that nobody would tell him matters of this kind. Was it that nobody told him or was it that he did not want to know? This was the point pressed by the astute Lord Lambton in the Profumo debate. My mind flashed back to my experiences some four years previously when, at the pinnacle of my prestige over the Mental Health Bill, I had been a guest at one of the more high-priority Downing Street tea-parties. I had been asked by my gracious host, Mr. Macmillan, whether I was satisfied with the provisions of the Bill then being debated in the House. Assuming that Mr. Harold Macmillan was genuinely seeking information, I had felt that this was my opportunity. There were many clauses in this Bill with defective provisions in regard to personal liberty and I endeavoured to say so. But I had not got very far on this before I was aware of a gesticulating figure in the background—it was Tony Barber, then, as it will be remembered, Private Secretary to the Prime Minister. It was clearly not done to tell the Prime Minister unpleasant truths.

Any information of any kind was, therefore, in vain as long as Mr. Harold Macmillan was still Prime Minister.

Mr. Macmillan had declared that he would stay. On the other hand 'the underground' had it differently. He was, so it was said, merely stalling, while still looking for a suitable opportunity to retire. But, if so, would he retire at the October Party Conference, or would he stay and lead the Party into the Election and retire after that? Answers to these two questions varied from day to day. It was not done, anywhere throughout the House of Commons, to discuss the Prime Minister's state of health. My political sense on the one hand told me that Mr. Harold Macmillan would not go if he could possibly help it. On the other hand, though I can make no claim to have diagnosed Mr. Macmillan's illness, my clinical sense as a doctor told me that he would not stay the course. The sporting aspect of the situation started to appeal to me. I was reminded of the story once told me of that distant time in our social history when life insurance could be taken out in casual fashion on the lives of other people and of the 'wise woman' in the Welsh mining village whose hobby it was with unerring instinct to put a bob on this or that neighbour who had started to fail.

I would put my bob on Mr. Macmillan.

Thus, I have the following statements on the record in reply to the recurring questions from the Press as to whether I had changed my mind or not.

30th June: *The People*—'I do not take seriously the Prime Minister's statement that he intends to remain. I am convinced that he will resign in the face of growing opposition. But, if he stays, I go. I cannot conduct an election campaign under his leadership. I would lose my self-respect.'

2nd July: At Edward Martell's meeting at the Caxton Hall I announce that, of the three telegrams and twenty-nine letters which I have received, the three telegrams and twenty letters approve my stand—as indeed they did. The disapproving letters were mainly anonymous. If 'Woman Conservative, Edinburgh' or 'Disgusted, Workington', had given their names, they would have carried more weight.

1st August: I repeat, after a further meeting with the Carlisle Conservative Executive that if Mr. Harold Macmillan was still the leader of the Party at the election, I would not contest my seat.

26th September: 'While I still sympathize with Mr. Macmillan in his difficult situation, I consider that the final responsibility for the conduct of the Prufumo affair lay at the Prime Minister's door.'

2nd October: I confirm that the Denning Report, just published, makes no difference to my position or my opinions.

In the *Sunday Express* of 6th October 'Cross-Bencher' reviewed the position in his customarily happy fashion. In the course of this he concluded that only three backbenchers were prepared to carry opposition to Mr. Harold Macmillan to the ultimate point. These are Lord Lambton, Mr Nigel Birch—and myself.

I could wish no better political epitaph.

The evening prior to my statement on 1st August, I had met the Executive of the Carlisle Conservative Association in all its panoply of some twenty to thirty people. In reply to protesters present I made a long explanation. I must have spoken for some forty-five minutes to these disturbed people, explaining with such lucidity as I could muster all the matters which I have set down in my previous chapters and which had occasioned my opposition to the Prime Minister. But I was uncomfortably aware that I was making little impression. It was not so much that my audience disagreed with what I was saying, as that they simply did not understand what I was talking about.

CHAPTER THIRTEEN

A BUNGLED JOB

*'It is the duty of the politician to tell the truth,' Mr.
Iain Macleod, defending his famous 'Spectator'
article to the Enfield West Conservative Association,
February, 1964.*

(1)

MR. HAROLD MACMILLAN went at last. As history records,
his enlarged prostate overtook him when, in defiance
of the opinion of many of his colleagues and against all
omens to the contrary, he was about to leave for the Annual
Conservative Conference at Blackpool on Tuesday, 8th
October, to announce his intention to lead the Conservative
Party at the forthcoming Election. Unkindly, but irresistibly,
one was reminded of the fate of Herod.

And, of course, I went also. Six days later, after he had gone,
on Monday, 14th October, the Carlisle Conservative Association Executive, true to its flair for the ridiculous, in secret
meeting and in my own absence, passed the vote of 'No
Confidence' in me as its candidate at the next Election, which
effectively terminated my own career in the House of Commons.

'There is irony at least in the latest turn of events over Dr.
Donald Johnson's position,' comments the *Cumberland Evening
News* in the first of my several political obituaries which were
to appear in its columns.

I do not embark on this chapter without feelings of poig-
nancy and regret. The long drawn-out and distressing struggle

between the Carlisle Conservative Association and myself—
so destructive of personal friendships, so bitter in many of its
manifestations, so universally disastrous in its *dénouement* at
the General Election—flitted in and out of the papers in
sporadic fashion for a whole year. Whereas it is not so much
my intention to give a blow-by-blow account of a dead
contest as it is to explore that most delicate question of all in
representative democracy—the relationship of the Member of
Parliament with his constituency Association, I will perhaps,
in the process of so doing, be able to enlighten those of my
friends who, owing to the vagaries of treatment given by the
London Press to news from the North, missed instalments of
the story at the time.

Throughout their thirteen years of Government, this
question was to prove the Achilles heel of the Conservative
Party organisation in the country: it continued so until the end.

In the post-war reorganisation of the Party, it had been
established as one of the triumphs of the new democratic
spirit that 'the Conservative and Unionist Party should be
constructed so that it remains based on the long-prized
independence of Constituency Associations'. But fifteen years
had not gone by before even the sponsor of these reforms,
Sir David Maxwell-Fyfe (writing later as The Earl of Kilmuir)
in his *Political Adventure* was admitting that 'The trouble with
the post-1950 situation has been that many Associations
assumed a control over their candidates which in some cases
has been tyrannical. . . . Looking back with all the benefits
of hindsight I am not sure that this recommendation has had
a wholly beneficial effect on the Party fortunes.'

The briefest examination of the result in Carlisle relative
to that of the 1964 General Election as a whole, with its
Labour overall majority of only five, shows this to be an
understatement.

In the course of my last two chapters I have drawn attention
to the part played by a chairman of the Party as a *tertius
gaudens* in this relationship in the circumstances that arose
in 1963.

By and large, however, there is no more maligned place

than Conservative Central Office. In their *Parliamentary Election Manual** this body of high-minded people piously quotes Burke—'Your representative owes you not his industry only, but his judgment; and he betrays instead of serving you, if he sacrifices it to your opinion . . . authoritative instructions, which the Member is bound implicitly to obey, though contrary to the dearest convictions of his judgment and conscience, are utterly unknown to the laws of the land, and against the tenor of our constitution.' The *Election Manual* likewise warns, in connection with the altered circumstances of a constituency association financing an Election, that 'Now that the Association pays, it must not regard the candidate (or M.P.) as an employee or as one who is under some financial obligation'.

Unfortunately few constituency Conservative Associations can have read their own Manual. For the facts of life for a Member of Parliament supported by a Conservative Association are at almost total variance with these advices.

From the very start in Carlisle, even at a time when I was treated with the greatest fondness, I was left in no doubt as to my status—I was 'the hired man', to be hired or fired conditional on my good behaviour, which could, of course, be interpreted in various ways. Various formulae are available to bring an M.P. into line from any deviation. A word spoken by him out of place and, if he is not 'upsetting the Party workers', then he is 'alienating supporters': or maybe both.

In my own case, it was both. It was not that I held opinions; it was that I failed to keep these opinions to myself.

'It is out of place for a back-bench M.P. to make a statement such as this,' declared the President of the Carlisle Conservative Association, the secretary of a wholesale grocery firm, consequent on my Macmillan statement in June 1963.

'Dr. Johnson has always been an outspoken M.P. and within reason there is no objection to this. But it is, of course, an Association's duty to decide in this context what is reason-

---

* *Parliamentary Election Manual*, 11th Edition (Conservative Central Office, 1963), p. 9.

able and what is not,' said the Chairman of the Association, an auctioneer, at a later date.

The attitude of the Conservative Central Office, when a constituency crisis arises due to a quarrel between the Member of Parliament and his constituency Executive, is one of those mysteries of perpetual fascination to the political correspondent. The invariable reply from Central Office itself to any question is a ritual washing of hands—'we are neutral,' 'we have no right to interfere.' Invariably also this reply is greeted with a distressing scepticism. For the further question invariably arises whether, in the case of a rebel M.P., Central Office are always as aloof from the contest as they wish to pretend: or whether their view is made known by discreet phone call from Chairman at Headquarters to Chairman of Constituency Association. In such circumstances the much-vaunted 'independence of the constituency Associations' could become merely a cloak for secret control.

In the light of the activities of Lord Poole during the summer of 1963 in his capacity of Joint Chairman of the Party, there were many suggestions from probing journalists that I had been the victim of subterfuge. But I have little evidence to support such a suggestion. The most that my intelligence service was able to elicit was that, at the Blackpool Conference, my Association Treasurer, an insurance agent, went out of his way in the most gallant fashion to give the Vice-Chairman of the Party, Lord Aldington,* a lift in his car from the Conference Hall to the latter's hotel.

What my Association Treasurer may have said about me to Lord Aldington, if anything, and what Lord Aldington may have replied to him is, however, immaterial. For this was no cloak-and-dagger affair. The incitement to action against recalcitrants was open enough in the last desperate efforts of the Party leaders of the day to rally the machine behind the ailing leader.

'Let the faint hearts go their way,' declaimed Mr. Iain Macleod, still Joint Chairman of the Party with Lord Poole, speaking to the Party Conference at Blackpool in October,

* Previously Sir Toby Low, Conservative M.P. for Blackpool (South).

'whoever they may be, there is no room for them in our Party. We are better without them.'

'The Conservative Party is like dry tinder and a spark will set it ablaze,' he said earlier in the same speech.

Here was the latter-day 'red glow on Skiddaw' to 'warn the burghers of Carlisle'. Mr. Iain Macleod (so soon to become a 'faint-heart' himself) might as well have mentioned me by name.

★　　★　　★　　★　　★

'I have to inform you that the Executive of the Association have passed a vote of no confidence in you as their candidate for the next Election,' said the Chairman of the Carlisle Association, when, at 9.30 p.m. at night, he phoned me after the meeting on Monday, 14th October, to give me this glad news. (He was good enough to confirm it in just those words in the letter which he wrote me next day).

I phoned Henry Kerby to tell him the news.

'But they're mad!' exclaimed Henry.

Of course they were mad. (My majority at the 1959 Election had been 1998 votes, the Labour majority in Carlisle in 1966 is now 4927.)

But those who dwell in 'the world of Jurgen's grandmother', have little insight into their own condition. Their action, in which they brought discredit to both themselves and the Conservative cause throughout the country, owing to their passing 'sentence'—and a political death sentence it was—on me, unheard and in my absence, was contrary to natural justice and fair play. (Just what the Conservative Party so sententiously condemns when it occurs in Labour and Trade Union circles!) But though it made little sense to anybody else, it made good sense to them within the context of their own reasoning.

There were those in the Carlisle Association with a long

history of political pugnacity who believed in getting their blow in first. In this they were successful. Above all, they wanted to shut me up. In this they were not so successful. As 'an execution squad' they bungled the job. There is the grisly story of medieval times associated with the Tower of London concerning the unfortunate Countess of Salisbury, whom the executioner had to chase round the block three times with his axe before he finally finished his job. That is the only parallel that I can think of. They were to finish me in the end, but it was a messy job.

However, as I search my conscience, I must not hold myself entirely blameless for what happened in Carlisle on the evening of 14th October 1963.

Had I still been a keen and tenacious Member of Parliament, finding my Parliamentary seat of value to me and determined to hold it at all cost, I might have acted differently in many ways. But, as readers of my story will have gathered, I was fed up. I did not care whether I stayed or went.

This feeling had not been assuaged by my interview with the Executive of the Carlisle Association on 31st July. I was tired of talking to them. At the end of that meeting I had actually suggested that, when they next met, they should discuss the matter by themselves. Then, it being the Parliamentary Recess, I went away and forgot about them. It seemed the best thing to do.

So, when it came to the crunch and to this meeting so opportunely timed for the Monday after the Conservative Party Conference at Blackpool, I was not at my most alert from a political point of view. Subsequent to an incident at Brighton in 1958 when, despite my work on the subject, I had been 'smothered' in connection with a resolution on mental health, I had lost my zest for Party Conferences—in any case, for an M.P. they are a 'busman's holiday'—it was no thrill to travel to Brighton, to Blackpool, to Scarborough or to Llandudno, to listen to the same Ministers to whom one was compelled to listen all too often throughout the weary year at Westminster. Hence, I was not at Blackpool and I must leave it to others to bear witness to the psychotic episode in the Party's history which supervened, in the leadership struggle that followed the retirement of Mr. Harold Macmillan. On this occasion, moreover, I had an alternative venue. The week of the Conservative Party Conference coincided with the week of the Frankfurt Book Fair and it was to the Frankfurt Book Fair I chose to go in the interests of my publishing firm— it was, in fact, at 8 a.m. on Frankfurt Station following an overnight journey from Paris that I bought the *Daily Telegraph* to see the headline news of Mr. Harold Macmillan's retirement.

On my arrival home late Saturday evening, I was tired from travelling, I had a cold and, following my Continental trip, publishing seemed a far more interesting occupation than politics, anyway. Such was my frame of mind when, on Sunday morning, I phoned my Chairman in Carlisle.

I did so with a measure of reluctance. At last, so it seemed, it had come to the point when publishing and politics were incompatible occupations.

'I expect that we can look at the matter differently now that Macmillan has gone,' I ventured rather half-heartedly.

'I don't know whether we can,' said my Chairman somewhat coldly.

A more tactful man would have seized his moment to jolly me along, but the tone in which he spoke provoked my most mischievous instincts. If I was really looking for someone to throw me out, here, I sensed, was my man.

However, for the moment, I contented myself with explaining to him that I had a cold and could not travel to Carlisle. Perhaps he would accept a statement for the following evening? He invited me to phone his secretary in the morning and what I had to say would be taken down on a dictaphone.

I pondered my statement throughout Sunday. As I did so, it came back to me forcibly that the staying or the going of Mr. Macmillan was, after all, not the main issue as far as I was concerned. The point to which my mind returned was the lot of the Government backbencher. Would I be in better straits under another leader, or in another Parliament, than those of which I had been complaining for years? I suspected from the tone of my Chairman's voice that the machine which he represented was wound up to destroy me—that possibly my fate had been determined while Harold Macmillan was still the leader and that, in the confusion following his retirement, those at the head of the Party—if at that juncture the Party could be said to have any head—had overlooked so minor a matter.

I might conceivably have avoided my fate by rushing up to Carlisle, presenting myself in a suitably grovelling attitude and saying something quite different from what I actually did say. But what then? I would merely find myself back at 'square one' in my original struggle. The statement which I wrote was a polite one (it is reproduced in full in Appendix I), but I made it clear that I would like to clarify my position as a backbencher before pledging loyalty to any future leader.

I thought that I heard my Chairman's secretary gasp slightly as she took down what I said. In any other walk of life this would have been a reasonable request. But 'in the world of Jurgen's grandmother', it was not a reasonable request. It was treachery of the basest sort, disloyalty already to another leader—even though, prior to the final choice of Sir Alec Douglas-Home, the Party did not have a leader. I had signed my own political death warrant.

My 'intelligence' at this meeting subsequently informed me that the Chairman, far from adopting a judicial attitude, gave a lead against me right from the start.

* * * * *

Mine was now the martyr's crown and maybe I should have been satisfied with this.

But, alas, that such mortification of the flesh was not possible for me without an accompanying feeling of resentment that the action of the Carlisle Executive was authoritarian and dictatorial. I had entered politics to fight for freedom—'to set the people free' as the old-time slogan had it. It was in my blood to resist this with all my might and main: and I would give them a run for their money.

A reference to my statement printed in Appendix I, of which they had disapproved so heartily, will show that all I had sought was reasonable discussion of the position of the back-bench Member of Parliament. This was the issue on which, allegedly anyway, I was eliminated. Reasonable discussion was what I sought: reasonable discussion was what I was denied.

How far would this refutation of reason, this denial of elementary human rights for a Member of Parliament, go? Curiosity for this interesting piece of political research was now my main motivation and I was my own guinea-pig for the purpose of the experiment.

My first gambit was the obvious one. I threatened to resign forthwith and to cause a by-election. It need scarcely be mentioned that, in October 1963, a by-election in Carlisle would have been highly inconvenient for the Conservative Party. 'Second Luton a Possibility' (the Luton by-election had just resulted disastrously for the Conservatives) declared the headline to an article by Ian Waller in the *Sunday Telegraph*.

But from my point of view it was simple. All I had to do, so I ascertained, was to drop a letter in the post to Mr. Speaker saying that I was applying for that convenient office of profit under the Crown, the Stewardship of the Chiltern Hundreds, and I would be rid of the lot. The temptation to do so forthwith was almost irresistible. But I restrained myself. I announced that I would wait until the opening of Parliament in order 'to clear up outstanding obligations'. My private intentions were to wait to see what happened during that time.

Much did happen. My threat, announced within forty-eight hours of the Executive's decision, made a certain impact. For the first time ever—the only time ever—I found myself sitting in the office of the Chairman of the Party in Smith Square. The Chairman of the Party, following reorganisation of the senior posts by Sir Alec Douglas-Home, who was now Prime Minister, was Lord Blakenham. Ten years previously (as I have recorded earlier in this book), as plain John Hare, M.P., and Vice-Chairman, he had befriended me and assisted me to obtain the nomination in Carlisle, subsequent to my interview with him when Central Office still occupied back rooms in Victoria Street. Over the years I had felt gratitude and a measure of admiration for this spry, decisive man who had leant over backwards to be fair to me when a difficult personal situation had arisen.

I hoped perhaps for a solution from this talk with Blakenham, who had proved so reasonable on my previous official encounter with him: but it was quickly clear that I had hoped in vain. Friendly as ever, he offered me a cigar. But somehow or other, in the more lush surroundings of Smith Square, it seemed to me that the virtue had gone out of him.

'We must think of the Party,' he admonished à propos of nothing in particular. I sensed that he was embarrassed by decisions of his predecessors in office, which he could not reveal. 'But it depends on the local people, as you know,' he added.

Whether the same admonition was given to 'the local people' in Carlisle or not, I do not know. But, whether it was or not, these extraordinary people, while arrogating the right to speak in the name of the Party, made it clear that, as far as they were concerned, they would as soon see the Party lose the seat as even talk reasonably.

'We are prepared for a by-election at any time,' said the agent in Carlisle to the Daily Express. This was the only public statement emanating from Carlisle at that time that can be traced.

It was left to me, the rebel and the dispossessed, to think of the Party!

As the opening of Parliament approached at the end of October, my affairs were wound up and I was ready to go. But, as might be expected, colleagues at Westminster, both Harold Gurden and Tom Iremonger,* were interceding with me and with those in high office. (Talk of 'pressures' may be discounted. I was already pressurised out of political existence.) Moreover, encouraging messages of support were coming to me from my friends in Carlisle, Jack Harrison and John Lett, whose staunch support was to mean much to me

* T. L. Iremonger, Conservative M.P. for Ilford (North).

in the coming months and about whom I could only wish
that I had space to say more.

Perhaps it was, after all, thought of the Party, perhaps it
was a sense of fairness to my own reputation that influenced me.
For indications also started to reach me that members of the
Carlisle Association Executive, experiencing some difficulty in
producing any sensible reason for their decision of 14th
October, were starting to hint that, behind the reserve of
secrecy, behind the formal reasons that had been made public,
were other and more cogent reasons for their action which
were so secret that they could not be revealed. Such rumours,
started in this way, needed no fanning. It was clear that,
provided that I could find a face-saving formula for with-
drawing my threat of resignation, I must stay and fight this
thing through.

I was enabled to do this by taking advantage of that rule
of the Carlisle Conservative Association which provided for a
special meeting of the Association on the demand of fifty
members for a stated purpose. I announced that, if I got fifty
signatures to a petition for such a meeting, I would retain my
seat until the end of the existing Parliament.

I had to get the majority of my own signatures. But, by dint
of several visits to Carlisle, I did so and by 1st December John
Lett, as sponsor of the petition for the meeting, was able to
present this to the Vice-Chairman of the Association. (The
Chairman, it is perhaps worth mentioning, had gone off to
New Zealand for a personal visit lasting several weeks.)
My signatures were obtained amidst a genuine wave of
popular support, even enthusiasm; for others besides myself
were beginning to find the secrecy of the Carlisle Conservative
Association tiresome. (Even the game of golf was temporarily
forgotten!)

I thus secured the right to an open hearing of my case
before the Association as a whole—a right which in any
properly conducted democratic community should have been
mine without the indignity of an M.P. having to beg round
for it from house to house on November evenings.

For the psychology that had motivated the action of the

Carlisle Executive in November had been vindicated. Though their sudden blow had created nothing but bewilderment locally, in an age of negative reactions it had been accepted without protest. The Press moreover had not been helpful. I regret to comment that it was just those newspapers which are continually taunting M.P.s for subservience and lack of independence who were ready with the most telling jibe when such independence encountered difficulties. Those headline writers again! 'SACKED M.P.' is, I imagine, the ideal head-line—it is short, pithy, it has punch and the requisite touch of malice. But it is totally inaccurate inasmuch as an M.P. cannot be sacked during his term in Parliament and is not, in any case, the employee of his local association. A fortunate modern trend, as in the case of Mr. Wolridge-Gordon, M.P. in East Aberdeen, and Commander Anthony Courtney in East Harrow, has shown that, when strife arises, the Constituency Executive can be 'sacked' rather than the M.P. But, prior to 1963, too many M.P.s had allowed themselves to be disposed of too easily and here was the SACKED M.P. headline in the *Daily Express* of 16th October and 18th November—and it was to continue through the coming months in a wider variety of papers until eventually quelled by threat of legal action. But this was not before the newspaper placards through Carlisle had been plastered with it.

So, when the Carlisle Conservative Executive in its wisdom, fixed 30th December for the date of the open meeting of the Association (this date was within the discretion of the Associa-tion Executive to fix), I sensed that, despite the congratulations and good wishes which at that moment surrounded me, I was already a dead duck.

They had once again caught me out. For my campaign, inevitably waged as an absentee and an occasional visitor to the constituency and so through the medium of the Press, automatically collapsed as the Christmas season approached and political acrimony gave way to messages of goodwill in the columns of the local papers.

None the less, when I entered the Association meeting in the Ballroom of the County Hotel, Carlisle, at the platform end of the room on the evening of 30th December, I received a shock. It is a scene engraven on my memory. The small band of cheering enthusiasts occupying a segment of the front benches were far outnumbered by the majority of the considerable audience of two hundred people—rather more than twice the number of people I had seen at any previous meeting of the Carlisle Association—who sat grim, silent and unmoved by my entry. I recognised instantly that my enemies were all present—not one was missing: but where were the encouraging people who but a month previously had greeted me at doors, who had shaken me by the hand in the streets, telling me that 'I had done a lot of good for Carlisle' and wishing me well? They, as far as I can gather subsequently, were all being visited by aged relatives who could not be left.

This was indeed no vindication meeting, but a 'Peoples' Court' that I had let myself in for. The Chairman spoke— and he spoke first—in damnatory fashion as if he were a public prosecutor. He had little to say that has not already been put down in these pages. Though it is interesting to recall that, high up on his list of indictments, was that I was endeavouring to force the appointment of an Ombudsman on the Government. Then, though I had repeatedly been censured myself for not maintaining secrecy, he had no hesitation in using against me the talk at the private dinner party after the 1959 Election at which I had been the host. The letter which I reproduce in Appendix I had, apparently, been 'the last straw'. The acclamation with which this statement was greeted made it clear to me, if it had not been clear before, that I had had it.

My reply in these circumstances was less than tactful. It was too good an opportunity to miss. For once in my life I could tell an audience what I thought of them—all the things that I had been longing to say for months. I must leave my reader to imagine what these were: suffice it that I took advantage of my opportunity. For I was a loser anyway. For instance, there were the young men in the two back rows, who started to stamp their feet after I had been speaking some forty minutes, and whom I had not seen before at any

Conservative Association meeting. It had been agreed that the ranks of the Carlisle Conservative Association should remain open for recruitment right up to the day of the meeting and I had endeavoured to mobilise my own support by writing a circular letter to those numerous people I had helped in various ways throughout my time as M.P., in some cases helped considerably, suggesting that they might join the Association. (It was a slight misfortune that one of these letters was sent in error to a Labour Councillor, who repaid his debt of gratitude to me for my help by sending it to the local Press with derisory comments!) When I had heard that recruiting to the Association had quickened during December I had flattered myself that it was the result of my efforts. But my enemies had done the same thing as I had and had done it with greater success. Did the presence of these young men and the fact that certain officers of the Association were closely associated with the Carlisle Rugby Football Club have any association with each other, I wondered?

The vote was taken. It was a heavy defeat—138 to 31 against me. They were a noble thirty-one, some of whom boldly faced the antagonistic gathering and spoke up on my behalf. But they were nineteen fewer than the people who had signed the original petition for the meeting!

The Executive ended up by threatening to resign *en masse* if the meeting did not support them. (Such was their loyalty once again to the Party!)

However, they won and I gave them a valediction:

'Your problems will be greater than mine.'

So it has proved to be.

(2)

On 24th January 1964, within a month of the Carlisle meeting, I resigned the Conservative Party Whip in Parliament, having decided to sit for the remainder of my time there as an Independent Member.

On announcing my resignation from the Party I issued the following statement:

'The Conservative Party is clearly undergoing a great sickness. In its present state of mental agony it is allowing itself to be tortured by ghosts.

'On all sides during the past four months I have encountered nobody but Rip Van Winkles still living in the days of Mr. Harold Macmillan.'

This is also true, to a large extent, three years later.

I gave in my resignation with regret and sorrow. This was intensified by the fact that my grievance against the Party Whip was not a personalised one in any way. As I have already indicated in Chapter Seven I had seen much of Martin Redmayne, Chief Government Whip during the 1959–64 Parliament. Indeed the intractable problems which have been the central theme of this story had been the occasion of regular discussion in a long succession of visits to the Chief Whip's Office over the years. I am sure that, within the limitations of his position, which under the Premiership of Mr. Harold Macmillan I cannot think to have been a very satisfactory one, Martin did his best for me. Eventually a cheerful sort of 'cop and robber' relationship had sprung up between us, one scarcely flurried even in the tensest moments.

Wisely, I think, Martin Redmayne did not try to lay down the law to me. This was left to the Chairman of the Carlisle Conservative Association, who at the Carlisle meeting on 30th December did so in clear and unambiguous terms.

'A Member of Parliament undoubtedly has complete freedom during his period of office,' said the Chairman, 'but such freedom carries responsibilities.

'When an Association are considering whether to readopt the sitting Member as their candidate at the next Election, it is surely reasonable for them to consider that Member's actions and words during his period of office.'

Words such as these (which represented the unspoken thoughts of many a more reticent constituency chairman throughout the country) arrogated power over a Member of

Parliament far beyond anything which the Party Whips had
ventured to claim throughout the whole of my own association
with them. This was power of a kind that would effectively
prevent any M.P. who wished a continuation of his time in
Parliament, either deviating from the Party line as interpreted
by the Officers of his Association, or indeed of saying anything
that would render him, in the opinion of his constituency
Executive, liable to public criticism in any other way.

Yet, despite the inference of such claims as this on the
position of the Member of Parliament, no word of protest
had been forthcoming from any direction. Indeed, since the
Carlisle Association not only received full support from the
Conservative organisational machine and from Conservative
Ministers during the Election, but also still remains affiliated
to the main body of the Party, it must be assumed that, despite
any assertions to the contrary, this is the correct interpretation
of the situation of a Member of Parliament in the Conservative
Party.

That is how I read it at the time and I felt it incumbent on
me to make a protest. Resignation from the Whip was the only
one available to me.

* * * * *

I can fairly claim that, throughout my eight years in
Parliament thus far, there had been few Members with a
better record of attendance than myself, with all the irksome
restrictions of personal freedom that this involved. Now the
sudden freedom to come and go at Westminster, thanks to
attaining my independence, was a most precious boon.

Apart from any other consideration, the sudden death on
4th September 1963 of my 'pair', Bill Williams, had been the
occasion of abiding grief to me. Throughout the long parliamentary terms over eight years, Bill and I had travelled home
together to Sutton three and four nights a week and in this
way had become an integral part of each other's lives. An
arrangement of mutual convenience had matured during

this time into a personal relationship motivated by feelings of respect.

In the words of the *Daily Telegraph* obituary notice:

'Mr. Williams, 68, is a distinct loss to the Opposition Front Bench. He was regarded as a potential Speaker in event of a Labour Government. He had the confidence of both sides of the House where he had sat since 1945. Amongst his characteristics were unfailing courtesy and a respect for the dignity of Parliament.'

More than that, Bill Williams was a dedicated man, an unceasing and tireless worker for the public good, whose devotion to Parliament had been repaid in poor coin. When the Conservative Establishment in 1959 had tentatively offered the Speakership to the Labour Party, Bill Williams' candidature had been specifically excluded by their insistence on a lawyer.

Now, after slogging on as a devoted constituency Member for a further five years, sudden death had come to him with a heart attack just as he was about to leave home to visit his Manchester constituency. His obituary notices were short: the extent and the depth of his qualities were almost totally unrecognised.

It occurred to me that it could well be the same with me. Come to think of it, my own record for voting and attendance had counted little enough for virtue when it came to the showdown. I might have saved myself much time and discomfort and my dear wife much loneliness had I taken those underlinings on the weekly Whip less seriously than I actually had done over the years. Now, so it had seemed, I might go on, sacrificing time and leisure and, at the end of the day, I too could drop dead in just such circumstances as those in which Bill Williams did. It was a sombre thought.

However, from February 1964 until the end of Parliament, I was able to exercise my freedom to come and go. Somehow, now that I was not compelled to be there, Parliament itself seemed different—I could look on it with fresh eyes. My former Party colleagues did not take my 'independence' too seriously: while, on my side, I can fairly claim that I was to be found in the Conservative lobby at any such time as urgency for my vote arose. Now that I was going, I started to take to the place: and it seemed that even the place itself, resentful of attempts at outside domination, after all this time started to take to me. I was, incidentally, the recipient of more than one constituency 'horror story' from my colleagues, all of them resembling in some respects my own.

Carlisle too started to look different. I regret to have to inform the Officers of my former Association that it was some relief to me too, to be able to visit Carlisle and not to have to see them, and to be able to express my opinions when I felt like it without being continually checked up on.

Freedom is exhilarating stuff. When, after a few weeks during which the morale of my local friends recovered from our defeat at the 30th December meeting, voices started to beckon once again from Carlisle with the siren song that I might fight the forthcoming General Election as an Independent Candidate in opposition to the candidate chosen by the Conservative Executive, I was not as deaf to this as I might have been. When, as the year of 1964 went on and the Election date was postponed by Sir Alec Douglas-Home, now Prime Minister, from May until October, it seemed that the position was worth testing and that there was time and opportunity for this.

★　　★　　★　　★　　★

Once again, during the summer days of 1964, we were out canvassing round the doors of Carlisle.

The simple question asked was: did the people of Carlisle want me to stand as an Independent Candidate at the General Election on the basis of my record as their Member?

Of course, they did. That was their clear verdict as we 'missioned' from door to door.

Half of the people—the Labour half—were naturally only too eager to see two Conservative candidates in the field; many of them were enjoying the entertainment offered by this non-stop row between the Association and myself; while quite a number were actually and genuinely at that stage on my side. The evidence seemed overwhelming, during this time when I was the only campaigning candidate, that I would obtain substantial support.

Having obtained some six hundred signatures to nomination papers, I announced on 16th September that I would stand as 'Conservative Independent' Candidate in the forthcoming General Election, which was, by now, fixed for 15th October. The Carlisle Conservative Executive were, as might be expected, right on the ball with a statement about what they termed my bid for personal power. After announcing my candidature in Carlisle at mid-day, I drove up to London, to find their very latest diatribe of condemnation displayed on the news on the tape on the notice board of the Oxford and Cambridge Club.

But what did they expect? Is it to be assumed that, as long as Parliament retains any shred of its dignity or any breath of individual freedom remains, a Member of Parliament condemned to political extinction by an authoritarian decision will refrain from making his final protest to the electors if he has the personal resources to do so? The principles involved are surely as important as are to-day's blurred differences between the two Parties themselves. It is as well that, even if it is only to curb the headstrong spirit of those who are prepared to use the machinery of the Party for the assertion of their own egos, the situation should be tested occasionally.

It is as well too that, until such time as we reach the point of no return in our headlong decline into a nation of robots, it should be made clear that the individual is not always totally expendable at the whim of the committee men. The full text of the letter from the President and Chairman of the Carlisle Association (reproduced in Appendix II) which appeared in the *Cumberland News* of 10th September immediately following the announcement of my candidature will show what I mean.

Be all this as it may, surprise was the keynote of the situation when I announced my candidature. There was my own initial surprise, on entering the unexplored regions of politics where

I now found myself, to discover the number of people who now, for the first time, after a whole year in which this dispute had filled the papers, discovered to their dismay that there were two Conservative candidates in Carlisle and started to clamour that somebody ought to do something about it.

But this eventuality should have been thought of before and there was, of course, at this stage nobody to do anything about anything. I have already discussed the part, or the non-part, of Conservative Central Office and the Whips' Office in this episode. Already, long since, the peacemakers in London, my colleagues, Harold Gurden and Tom Iremonger, had done their best, only to meet the same 'helpless' attitude as I had done myself in the face of the obduracy of the Carlisle Conservative Officers. Nor perhaps was I the most co-operative person in these ventures: though I too had pro-pounded a solution when on 9th June I had unsuccessfully tried to introduce my Single Transferable Vote Bill to the House of Commons under the Ten Minute Rule.

In the face of all this, the General Election of 1964 in Carlisle was merely the final stage of an unmitigated tragedy moving inexorably towards its close. With uncomprising arrogance on one side, and my own equally obstinate individ-ualism on the other, as one Press observer remarked, all the Labour candidate had to do was 'sit tight' and let the Con-servatives destroy one another.

In my previous books I have been able to write in lively and amusing vein of elections in which I participated. There was, however, nothing either lively or amusing about this 1964 Election in Carlisle.

There are many people whom I have to thank—not least, Betty and the family, Norman and Carol, who cheerfully foreswore our usual summer holiday and trekked up to Carlisle to make our temporary home in the small semi-detached house in Moorhouse Road, from where the view over the old-fashioned industrial town reminded me so much of my child-hood days in Bury, Lancashire; and who worked hard through-out the campaign in lieu of gambolling on Continental beaches. There is also Anne Powell of Guildford who gave up her vacation as a student of London University and joined us. I have also to thank John Lett and the small band of volunteer helpers who rallied round me, either out of personal loyalty or from staunch faith in what I was endeavouring to represent. Throughout the day and late into the evening these good people worked hard, delivering my election address, kindly entertaining me, giving support and help at my meetings. No kudos accrues from the support of a failed Independent Candidate and I would probably embarrass them even in mentioning them by name: but I hope that they will realise how much I appreciate their unstinting support right up to the last sad moments of the campaign.

There are many too whom I have to condemn. But I must leave them to their own consciences, as they survey the ruins of their cause, to which they contributed so substantially by their own actions.

The story of the Election can be told briefly. The Johnson campaign started well. Indeed, it seemed that, as a result of my summer campaigning, I had converted the whole electorate of Carlisle to the thesis of the importance of the independence of their Member of Parliament. Betty and I could not spend an evening half-hour in any saloon bar in the town without sooner or later someone, amidst general murmurs of approval, coming up and shaking me by the hand with a commendatory remark 'I admire your principles, doctor'—an unusual demonstration for these customarily reticent people. (Undoubtedly, some of these spokesmen were Labour people, of course!) However, the atmosphere was such that some observers were already giving me 15,000 votes! REBEL DOMINATES CARLISLE ELECTION: DOCTOR'S BEDSIDE MANNER are the *Yorkshire Post* headlines on 1st October.

But, as the days went by, in the background it was not so happy. It became a sorry story of a spy planted on my Committee, defectors from my organisation leaving large gaps of work to be covered by already tiring faithful workers, victimisation of one of my supporters, attempts at intimidation of others, all on a sufficient scale to ensure failure to recruit

further to my Committee. Moreover, my official Party com-
petitors were entering the field, both of them, heaven help
them, declaring their own belief in the independence of a
Member of Parliament!

None the less, as the final day for Nominations approached
on Monday, 5th October, my campaign was still holding up
well. I was estimating myself to gain between 5,000 and 15,000
votes and I do not think this was an unfair estimate at the
time. Insurance agents going from door to door, mobile shop
van drivers, those who should be in the know, were stopping
me in the street to tell me that I was winning. I even began to
worry—the thought haunted me that in a couple of weeks
time I would find myself back in Parliament, as an Independent
perhaps, but one not taken very seriously. My friends would be
particularly friendly; there would be intercessions and the
intercessions would result in a cosy chat with Martin Redmayne
—it would be just like old times and, hey presto, I would be
back spending my afternoons and evenings in the Interview
Rooms' passage again!

But I need not have worried.

A detailed account of subsequent events is redundant except
in as much as it can throw light on reasons for the total
elimination of Independent competition for Parliamentary
seats. But there is one episode that cannot be glossed over
since, as far as I was concerned, it formed the climacteric of
the Election.

It had been the feature of the two previous General Elections
in Carlisle which I had contested in 1955 and 1959, that,
though there had been many Liberal votes available, there
had been no Liberal candidates in the field. I had owed my
original victory in 1955 to the fact that the 6000 votes which
had been cast for the Liberal candidate in 1951 had mainly
split my way in a proportion of 5 to 1. There were rumours
of Liberal candidates and there were, in fact, prospective
Liberal candidates, but, when it came to the point, the
Liberals had never had any money with which to fight the
Election. So it was now in 1964: the Liberals had already
announced that they would not fight the Election: and there

was no doubt where the main body of my support was coming from in these early stages of the campaign—this was from the Liberal vote. With a Liberal vote of 4000 to 5000 behind me plus my own Conservative supporters, I was a formidable threat to the Conservative Executive.

It was the Saturday morning prior to Nomination Day on the Monday that, as we drove through Court Square, we spotted the Association's sole Life President with glowering mien on the opposite side of the road: we knew from experience that, when the Association's sole Life President looked like that, it usually boded someone or other no good.

As late as the morning of the following day, Sunday, I made a final check up of the principal signatories of my nomination papers, some of them Liberal sympathisers, and there was still no Liberal candidate. It was only on the Sunday evening local TV news that there came the announcement, originating from outside the constituency—it was to the effect that somehow, at this very last moment, the money had been found and there would after all be a Liberal Candidate.

The following morning Mr. Brian Ashmore was nominated as Liberal Candidate. There were strong denials that this money which had suddenly appeared (and which failed to manifest itself either at the previous two elections or at the subsequent one in 1966) was 'Conservative money', but its source has not been revealed from that day to this. I still seek enlightenment.

Mr. Brian Ashmore too was a firm believer in the independence of a Member of Parliament: and expressed his admiration for my principles in the most enthusiastic fashion whenever we ran into each other during the subsequent days. None the less, a person of no mean eloquence in his own interest, he knocked the bottom out of my chances of obtaining any substantial vote.

*   *   *   *   *

But why continue with a distasteful story? I do so only

out of the sternest sense of obligation as a recorder of the time in which I live. One of our Sunday political commentators (I think it was William Rees-Mogg in the *Sunday Times*) has suggested that in Britain we may well lose our freedom, while still possessing all its outward historic signs and trappings, such as the Parliament at Westminster, contested elections and so on. We are perhaps half-way to this point when two Party political machines, both standing for much the same policies even though their respective members have different social origins, can between them eliminate completely every single serious competitor at the polls.

I have hinted at intimidation and gaps in my organisation as a consequence of 'approaches' to my supporters. Now, scarcely a day passed without one or the other of my friends receiving a visitation from one of the Officers of the Carlisle Conservative Association, or maybe two or three of them together. Canvassing is, of course, an entirely proper activity at British elections, nor can I complain of anything improper being said by these visitors, but the effect of this sombre cortège on the morale of many of those visited was, of course, considerable.

But victimisation was not absent. One of my supporters, Mr. Tommy Hunter, was expelled from the Denton Holme Conservative Club consequent on an admission that he had once been a member of the Labour Party—a peccadillo that would almost certainly have been overlooked in normal circumstances. In fact, there are those who say that the membership of this club might well be decimated if such a test was rigidly applied.

Little wonder that, as the days went on, our friends were showing a tendency to visit us more and more after dark!

The ballot is secret. But in some 5 per cent of the votes cast in Carlisle the ballot was not secret at all. For, as a result of a heavy round up of invalids and elderly people, no less than 2500 electors were listed as postal voters. In this procedure identity has to be witnessed—a complex procedure for elderly people, usually resulting in votes being overseen as well. Such votes are customarily these days regarded as the 'property' of the Party which has recruited them. As amateur organisers, we had marvelled at the eagerness and impatience of the professional Party agents to get their hands on the roll of postal voters issued by the Returning Officer during the last week of the campaign, but soon we appreciated the reason for this. Evidence of deliberate intimidation of one such vote—an elderly lady in hospital—was brought up at one of my meetings. I took this to the Returning Officer, but the Returning Officer could give me no remedy. My remedy was that of an electoral petition, an expensive procedure that could only be initiated after the election and was only valid in the event of the result being a close one. I announced this to the Press, but contemporary comment from the Conservative agent was: 'This is just another of Dr. Johnson's scares.'

I did, of course, enjoy unfettered freedom of speech throughout the campaign. Indeed, I held a series of meetings at which I put my message over without molestation in any way. There were attendances of ten at one, eight at another, twelve at another, mainly composed of my own loyal supporters—there were scarcely a dozen fresh faces in all at the lot. This was not exactly a multitude to be swayed by one's eloquence.

During these final days of the Election, the national Press, which had been so interested in my doings hitherto, forgot about me and scarcely gave me a mention. Not so the local Press: for this was the letter which appeared in prominent type in the *Cumberland Evening News* on Tuesday, 13th October, two days before Polling Day.

I WAS DOCTOR'S AGENT

'I was Dr. Johnson's election agent when he was first elected a Member of Parliament for Carlisle. I was appointed by the Conservative Central Office, who also paid me, and it was not my task to question who was the candidate, or the personalities of the Carlisle Association.

'I now have nothing to do with the Conservative

Association, nor have I taken any professional interest in politics since those days, but as a result of my job there I do know quite a lot about Dr. Johnson.

'I would suggest that before any person casts a vote for him they look at his record before his election.

'My impression of him in those days was that he had a vast personal interest in his own publicity, and a very small opinion of the Conservative Party and, in particular, the Central Office. I think that impression has been proved by events during his period as an M.P.

'I very much doubt if he would ever have been elected if it had not been for the enormous amount of help, both active and financial, given by members of the Carlisle Association, in particular some whom he has named in his recent vendetta against the Association. The amazing part is that they put up with him for so long.

'My advice to any electors, if they will take it, is to vote Labour, Liberal or Conservative, according to your opinion, but for heaven's sake don't waste a vote.'

T. V. Rabbidge.

During the final week of the Election it is no exaggeration to say that I was effectively insulated from all but twenty or thirty immediate supporters.

Meanwhile my former friends of the Conservative Association were working a good deal harder against me than they ever did for me: it has ever been my misfortune that I am able to galvanise my enemies into frenetic activity! A new feature in Carlisle electioneering manifested itself in the shape of posters in luminous paint. Down the whole of the Brampton Road (the principal residential road of Carlisle) in which I cannot recollect my own photograph ever appearing, on either side large photographs of my official Conservative opponent, Mr. Peter Boydell, blossomed in such a manner as to make any entrant to this thoroughfare imagine that he

was entering the Fairy Glen in a fairground. Not to be outdone,
Labour posters in luminous red, supported on sticks and
staves, shot up, as if from dragons' teeth, in the gardens of
almost every second house throughout the Council estates.

It came to Polling Day and I had built up my own personal
list of calls to take voters to the polls. But, alas, I was wasting
my time—everyone on whom I called had either been or
was not ready to go and, by the time afternoon came, it was
fairly obvious that nobody wanted to be seen going to the poll
with me at all, however they might vote! My work was exhausted long before the Polls were closed. Attempts to rally
final individual votes proved a desperate failure. Intimidation
was by no means one-sided. Council estates which, even up
to a few days previously, I had known as friendly places, had
suddenly in the gathering darkness of this Polling Day turned
into luminous red-shining hells with large LABOUR-plastered
cars wending their way slowly up and down the narrow
alleyways and cul-de-sacs. Attached to each car were six to
eight 'storm troopers' with red rosettes and lists of 'knocking-up'
numbers. Apart from this there was not a soul about—it was
as if there was a curfew on and nobody could go out unless
they were conducted in one of these frightening vehicles.

As I drove back to our house in Moorhouse Road to wait
until close of Poll and the Count of Votes, I knew that my
electioneering days in Carlisle were over.

The count of votes at Carlisle's Covered Market was
something of a formality as far as I was concerned. Except
that, with a mere 1227 votes, I did even worse that I could
possibly have expected. At the end of all this effort I got no
more votes than if I had been a 'Flat Earth' candidate; I
would have obtained considerably more if I had stood as an
anti-vivisectionist. The Carlisle Conservative Association had
achieved their objective and had rubbed me out. Unfortunately, however, it was for them a *succès fou*, for there
emerged from the turmoil as the new M.P. for Carlisle, the
friendly smiling Mr. Ron Lewis, railway worker, the Labour
Candidate who believed in the Independence of the Member
of Parliament every bit as fervently as I did. Though I can

only hope, for his sake, that he does not have to put his belief to the test in the same way.

As for me, the Press were once again interested,

'What do you intend to do now, Dr. Johnson?' they asked.

I told them that I intended to write a book.

But nobody was particularly impressed by that.

NEVER GLAD CONFIDENT MORNING AGAIN

IT IS appropriate that I should write this Epilogue in order to bring the fortunes of the *dramatis personae* up to date these three years later at the time of going to press.

Can I say that 'they all lived happily ever afterwards'? Not entirely.

★　　★　　★　　★　　★

For myself, the writer, not to worry! It is a far happier life to breathe the air of freedom in quiet obscurity, to reflect leisurely on the lessons of a brief but crowded life in Parliament, than to remain a toothless lion, fretting in vain against the bars (however gilded) of the cage from which I escaped in such arduous fashion just as the final planks were being nailed together. No longer do I have to contemplate those chilly Friday evenings spent pacing No. 13 Platform on Euston Station, those equally chilly Saturday afternoons exposed to the north winds that ventilate the spectators' stand of the Carlisle United football ground (I am still happy to follow the waxing fortunes of this excellent team in the comfort of reading my Sunday morning paper): nor do I have to spend my Sunday, prior to a further week's incarceration at Westminster, sorting out a fistful of personal grievance cases on my return home.

On the contrary I am able to pursue my way in that personal freedom and comfort suitable to my age and station in life. If, at the same time, I am able still to have my say with the aid of my independent publishing firm, then that is all added unto me.

In any case, a new sense of compulsion possessed me in the final stages of my career. It was that, regardless of all else, I must find some respite from the distractions of the political struggle for the purpose of contemplation, to gather in the loose ends and to set my conclusions down on paper while I still possessed life and strength for that purpose, and before I too sank beneath the strain of frustrated endeavour, as had done my friends, Bob Crouch and Bill Williams, to whom I have paid tribute—these two were to be joined all too soon by my splendid companion, Norman Dodds, in his sudden death in August 1965 following a period of overstrain. All three of these noble people can surely be considered as martyrs to a system so completely destructive of the active-minded and the conscientious.

It is perhaps fortunate that my ambition did not extend beyond this and that I have had the independent resources to pursue it, as certainly my political destruction by the Committee men of Carlisle would have finished my chances of taking any other active part in the life of the community.

I have reproduced the Rabbidge-*Cumberland Evening News* letter, which was the culmination of the massive campaign of obloquy to which I was subjected in Carlisle, once I had decided, as an individual, to challenge the conspiratorial society and defy the Committee: and, though it was but the small portion of the iceberg which stood above the surface, it is an example of the type of personal defamation which anyone has to face in pursuing an individual course in this present day and age.

One must assume, in the light of the result of the Carlisle Election, that this will have 'deceived many' in the context in which it was published and read. It was only in the cool, unemotional light of British justice that it started to look different.

It was, of course, only fair that my detractors should be given the opportunity to substantiate the accusations which they brought against me. They were given just this opportunity with the initiation, at an early date after the Election, of the case of *Johnson* v. *Cumberland Newspapers Ltd. and Trevor V. Rabbidge* in the Queen's Bench Division of the High Court of Justice. They did not unfortunately take it. Indeed it will be no surprise to my reader to hear that silence continued to prevail for some eighteen months, punctuated only by the production of unhelpful documents forced by legal procedure from the reluctant defendants. Patience and my abiding faith in my excellent legal advisers prevailed, however, and eventually on 8th June 1966 Queen's Bench Court 7 was the scene of a brief drama in which the defendants' legal representatives participated to offer an apology as fulsome as had been the original libel. While the agreed damages at least paid a part of my election expenses.

Who, after all, can complain if 'the mills of the Gods grind slowly'? As T.E. ('Peter') Utley remarked almost simultaneously in his generous review in the *Daily Telegraph* of my firm's publication *Conspiracy* by Douglas Rookes (whose story of his quarrel with the officials of his Union bears so close a resemblance to my own), 'Government by law may have its disadvantages; it is preferable to Government by smear'. For it was this latter to which I had been subjected from the moment I had defied the power of the governing Establishment. Whether you fall foul of Trade Union officialdom, Government bureaucracy or Conservative committee, the treatment is much the same.

*   *   *   *   *

For the rest, I am reminded of that eerie little story of medieval Spain. Near the small town of Martos in Southern Spain there is the Pena de los Carvajales, the rock from which the two unjustly condemned Carvajal brothers were thrown to death by order of Ferdinand IV in 1312. They had protested their innocence and appealed to the judgment of God in thirty days. As the king died during that time, he was subsequently called *El Emplazado* (the one who is summoned). When, at the end of the meeting of the Carlisle Conservative

"Your problems are greater than mine"
(with acknowledgements to the Carlisle Journal: 3rd January 1964)

Association on 30th December 1963, I had uttered my forecast to this body that 'Your problems will be greater than mine', this remark was looked upon with mild derision. As a contemporary cartoon, which I reproduce from the *Carlisle Journal*, illustrates, it merely gave scope for the local satirists.

But who can now say, three years later, that I was wrong?

There is no need any longer to quote the political commentators verbatim, for there is scarcely a paper that one picks up which fails to put forward its own version on the debilitated state of the Conservative Party. When I resigned the Party Whip in January 1964, I spoke of 'the great sickness' of the Party. This strange wasting sickness has continued unabated since that date, defying all efforts at diagnosis from the multitude of political doctors that throng the bedside.

Frequently, under the stress of disaster, great truths emerge. Within a few days of the Profumo debate in June 1963 the *Daily Telegraph* editorial contained the following advice:

'The Conservative Party must regenerate itself, fashion itself anew. It must produce an alternative Government of its own. . . . This is like asking a patient to perform a painful and delicate operation on himself. Performed none the less it must be: otherwise we may be saddled with a Labour Government which may last for years and which may not be the anodyne affair which some expect.'

But the Party has shrunk from any such operation. Or worse still, may be, it has performed the wrong operation— a self-castration in which it had thrown overboard all traces of the dignity, the maturity of wisdom, the worldly experience and the political tolerance with which it was once endowed.

The Conservative Party, indeed, has changed. The ranks of the Old Etonians are thinning out: the knights of the shires are a dwindling company. The Old Establishment is already but a dim memory and has been succeeded by the New Establishment: in the choice of Parliamentary candidates the magic of the Old Etonian tie is replaced by the hypnotic compulsion induced by membership of the Bow Group and officership in a Young Conservative Association. It is the 'pore scholars' of Rab Butler and what one might term 'the

Bow ideal' of Harold Macmillan who have succeeded to the purple.

But the Press reports and Parliamentary commentators fortify one's suspicions.

'Open frivolity' chides *The Times*, referring to the behaviour of Conservative M.P.s, 'giggling silliness' comments the *Daily Telegraph*, both in the same week of July 1966.

'Why are the backbench Tories so feeble?' asks *Crossbow* simultaneously in despair.

In my search for truth I am reminded of another story. It is that of the young and inexperienced visiting lay preacher of the Methodist Church who had just given his address to a Sunday evening congregation in a remote Lancashire town. He was conscious that he had made a hash of things and he duly apologised at the end of the service.

'Nay, lad', comforted the senior steward of the church, "'tis not thee, 'tis chap as sent thee as we're after.'

Who, after all, is responsible for the composition of the parliamentary Conservative Party to-day, both as regards the selection of individual M.P.s by constituency associations and also to a large extent those originally selected for promotion to the Front Bench?

We have seen that it was Mr. Harold Macmillan. Here, three years after he has gone, the world of Mr. Macmillan's phantasies has come to life—the young, progressive, well-bred advocates of 'the Middle Way' are in the van of leadership.

To ascertain Party ills of the present, we must return to our final diagnosis of Mr. Macmillan. As one surveys the magnificent edifice which was presented by the political personality of Mr. Macmillan, who can fail to be impressed by its grand façade, its outstanding *pavillons*, its pepper pot turrets and its fine mansard roofs, but it is difficult to avoid the feeling that, somewhere or other, in some obscure but vital corner, there was not a slate loose which proved fatal to the whole structure.

In my Introduction I have referred to the tendency of mental confusion to spread in the closed world of the conspiracy. Such a tendency, for instance, is well illustrated by the so-called 'Famous Tate Affair', recently re-publicized by

Sir John Rothenstein in his autobiography *Brave Day: Hideous Night:* summed up by Lord Robbins, one of the then governors, as 'a case of collective madness'. Surely no other description than this can be given to the pattern of behaviour which the leadership of the Conservative Party presented during those distressing days of the summer of 1963 about which I have written—and, of course, subsequently during the leadership struggle at the Blackpool Conference in the same year.

Taking a comprehensive view of the course of events since July 1962, it is as if the captain of the ship had gone berserk and shot all the senior officers, leaving the cabin boys in charge, while most of the intermediary ranks and crew have been washed overboard, to fend for themselves as best they may. Yet the *s.s. Tory,* after striking the reefs of electoral defeat, lurches forward through the howling gales of Opposition as if nothing untoward had happened. Little wonder that it shows a pathetic inability to benefit from the mistakes of its opponents.

Let us face it. A gentle and mild-mannered man in his personal life, in his political behaviour Mr. Harold Macmillan showed a unique capacity for ruthlessness and destruction. A Lenin disguised as an Edwardian *roué,* he took the Conservative Party as he found it, tore it into small pieces and then, for good measure, tore those pieces into still smaller pieces again. While the Party, deceived by outward appearances, enmeshed in authoritarianism and misguided loyalties, submitted itself uncomplainingly to this process.

But it is, of course, more relevant to look at his positive aims, at which we have so far only glanced hurriedly in Chapter Five and in the accomplishment of which such considerable destruction was involved. With phantasies perhaps of 'a greater and a wider Eton', founded on the Bow Group and the Young Conservative Associations, it would seem that this revolutionary political scholar, looking for political inspiration, must have found it in the system of the Osmanli Turks of the Middle Ages of whom our own historian, Arnold Toynbee has written:

'Perhaps no more daring experiment has been tried on a large scale upon the face of the earth than that embodied in the Ottoman Ruling Institution. Its nearest ideal analogy is found in the Republic of Plato. The Ottoman system deliberately took slaves and made them Ministers of State. it took them from the sheep run and the plough tail and made them courtiers and the husbands of princesses.'*

This is mere speculation. But clearly the Macmillan ideal was to maintain the hierarchical system of Conservative government, yet to take its leaders from all classes of society *at an early age* and condition them to the demands of the organisation. The italicised words in my last sentence are the operative ones.

We are not to know how this would have turned out in Government had it been successful. But undoubtedly it would have perpetuated the worst aspects of Party authoritarianism of which I have had to complain and given rise to new forms of exclusiveness and conformity, meanwhile intensifying rather than breaking down the remoteness and monastic seclusion of the House of Commons; while it would have lost the better virtues of tolerance and liberal-mindedness, the wisdom and worldly experience brought into the seat of government by men of more mature years, successful in other spheres of life, and the *noblesse oblige* of aristocratic tradition. Thus exactly reversing the famous maxim of Disraeli.

Even though, trained in the art of what is now known as consensus politics, and of appeasing 'the middle of the road' voter, such a Party as this might well have kept a nominally Conservative Government in power from generation to generation, it would have formed a system totally alien to the traditions of liberal democracy and would have ensured the final demise of that freedom of which Conservatives like to talk and which they were originally elected to preserve.

However, in the transfer of power from his own hands to those of the next generation, the catch was muffed and the ball was dropped to the ground, from where it was picked up by

* *Study of History*, Vol. III, by Arnold Toynbee (Oxford University Press) p. 33.

that most adept of all the pupils of Mr. Harold Macmillan in political tactics, the second Harold, Mr. Harold Wilson.

Thus the phantasy world of Mr. Harold Macmillan is still but a world of shadow. For those who practise consensus politics in Government inevitably pay the penalty in Opposition. As is now comprehended by official Conservative propaganda, it is not to the advantage of any Opposition that the issues between the Government and itself should be blurred. While above and beyond this, there still persists the overhang of feelings of betrayal amongst the Party's more purist followers with the consequent sagging of morale.

Consensus politics is no mere academic term. Illustrations of it in practice have occurred throughout my story—Mr. Edward Heath with the Trade Unions, Mr. Iain Macleod with Africa, Mr. Enoch Powell with the National Health Service. And now, whatever language these men may use in Opposition, however the talk comes about 'the honest Party', or even of 'Freedom' and 'The Great Divide', it will inevitably raise the cynical smile and fail to convey reassurance amongst the disbelieving that they will act in any different way, should they find themselves once again in Government. Amongst these marginal people that is the most crucial question of all and it creates the doubt as to whether, following a spell of 'consensus government', an entire change of personnel at its head is needed before the defeated Party can find a sound basis from which to fight back.

Little wonder that, in ignoring these factors—in merely wishing its problems away and pretending that they do not exist—the Tory Party gives the impression that, while presuming to advise the solution of everybody else's problems, it has failed to solve its own. Stereotyped and impeccably dressed young men, young men who all look the same from wherever they may have come, step to the rostrum to talk about this and that issue, about freedom, liberty and regard for the individual. But they fail to make a case. For, on some scores, the Party, following their own years of Government, would have had to have done just what the Labour Government has done in the face of the wage inflation originally condoned by the attitudes of Macmillan Government: on yet other scores, the projects advocated should have been done by the Conservatives in Government when they had the chance but so recently.

Amidst the protestations of loyalty and unity and the standing ovations, it is as if the Party as a whole, with its knights of the shires replaced but by 'shadow knights', has been afflicted by the incurable disease of Liliputanism— the compulsive urge to grow smaller and less significant. It is as if, four years ago, Mr. Harold Macmillan had held out the mushroom temptingly labelled EAT ME and the Party, like Alice, has eaten it to find itself undergoing a diminishing process without knowing what is happening or when it is going to stop.

'The Conservative Party has never been in a more fundamentally adverse position than it is to-day', pronounced Mr. Ronald Butt in *The Financial Times* of 14th October 1966, coincident with the final day of the Conservative Party Conference.

At this stage we can only respectfully doff our hats and turn away from this heartrending scene.

*   *   *   *   *

Where shall we find the solution to the difficult problems that confront us at the present time. What are the proper answers? What, indeed, are the proper questions?

I do not find them amongst the political correspondants, preoccupied as these excellent gentlemen are with the battles of political faction. Nor with this brand of economic policy or that brand of economic policy at a time when, as a result of many years of consensus politics, the policies of the two Parties are virtually identical, one with the other, in an era when Conservative Government competes with Socialist Opposition on a 'Me Too' basis, and Socialist Government to save itself has to introduce traditional Conservative financial remedies for inflation.

Rather do I find the distant echo of my own story in Mr.

Geoffrey Owen's article 'Harvard's British Graduates: There's Little Encouragement to Come Home' in *The Financial Times* of Thursday, 8th October 1966.

'The job sounded good, but I was given no work to do. I spent all my time reading *Time* magazine.'

No, this is not a quote from myself or any other disgruntled M.P., but it is a selected comment which is attributed to one of a number of British business school graduates concerning his first job in British industry, which the author of the article compares unfavourably to the American interest in the potentialities of a new man in a corresponding job.

In the sphere of the Health Service, there is the paradox of shortage of doctors on the one hand and doctors spending their time doing the work of medical orderlies on the other.

Why are the doctors emigrating?

'At last, I am doing the work for which I was trained', writes back more than one successful medical *emigré*.

This is the most vital issue of our time, namely that the brains of our nation, whether business or professional, commercial or skilled artisan, should be put to constructive use before they are entirely drained away owing to disgust at stale custom, snobbism, exclusiveness or bureaucratic restriction, Party wrangles over minor nuances of legislation in which 'the mountains labour and a ridiculous mouse is born' are of minor importance compared with this.

I have one final story to tell. It is a background story to what I have already told about my Parliamentary frustrations. I was, after all, by no means a young man, but in my late fifties with many years of experience behind me when, by chance, I found myself one of a dinner party consisting mainly of senior doctors of the medical Establishment. In front of me, but without giving me any opportunity to intervene, they discussed the ills of the medical Establishment. They had one common 'moan'—namely, the paucity of medical personel for manning important committees. I have to ask my reader to relate this incident to the context of my Chapter Eight—the story of Harmony Hall, my Questions to the Prime Minister in regard to the appointment of M.P.s to Commissions and

Standing Committees. Here was I on the one hand, clamouring for useful and constructive work: here were these strange, self-contained people on the other, bemoaning in my actual presence the dearth of people with such qualifications as I had to offer. Between us, however, was the dead hand of 'the conspiracies'—the Ministry of Health bureaucracy, the Party machine of the Tory Party, with whom 'my face did not fit'.

★   ★   ★   ★   ★

'Under Mr. Heath we shall liberate the energies of the people', declared my Conservative M.P. in his Election Address in the 1966 General Election.

'Individual initiative, individual energy . . . new dynamism . . . fresh confidence . . . increasing efficiency . . . give the nation back its sense of achievement . . . give opportunities to all the pacemakers' —such, and other similar phrases, are amongst the torrent of words and exhortations that pour from Mr. Edward Heath.

But where is all this going to start, if not in the leading councils of the nation, in Parliament? How is it going to start while Parliament remains in the hands of the Party machines who set themselves to paralyse just those initiatives of which Mr. Heath talks?

Within these final pages is Appendix II—the explanatory letter from the Officers of the Carlisle Conservative Association issued in the local paper as to why they lost confidence in me. It was not only—as they are some pains to explain—because I criticised Mr. Harold Macmillan, but because I 'gave the impression that I considered the leaders of the Party were failing to appreciate my peculiar talents and qualifications', because I 'would not pledge my support to any new leader, whoever he might be, unless he agreed to fulfil certain conditions laid down by myself'.

Such was the language of hyperbole provoked by the statement of polite concern for 'the position and status of the back-bench Member of Parliament' in my own letter printed in the previous Appendix. Such concern is, indeed, justifiable, when the position of the back-bench M.P. under a Tory Government is the equivalent of Oliver Twist, the orphan boy bawled out because he asked for a second helping of porridge. My request had, you will recollect, been referred to by the Chairman of the Association as 'the last straw'.

It may well be thought that there is reasoning of a kind, if a somewhat authoritarian kind, in the letter of the President and Chairman of the Carlisle Association. That may be so, but that is not the point. The point is that that this reasoning does not equate in any way with the freedom language of Mr. Edward Heath and of my own Member of Parliament.

There can, moreover, be no washing of hands this time by the Central Conservative Party, and no passing the buck to the local Party. For when it came to the crunch at the General Election in October 1964, these words and these attitudes were implicitly supported by Ministers and by M.P.s (regardless in some instances of personal friendships) on platforms; they were supported too by the Conservative Party organisation in the various forms of help given to my 'officially' adopted opponent. There was moreover no appeal from this local authoritarianism, so completely backed by the weight of central organisation: when such was attempted by my principal supporter in Carlisle, Mr. John Lett, it was entirely scouted by Lord Chelmer, Chairman of the National Union of Conservative Associations. The Party as a whole cannot therefore divest itself of its responsibility.

The stark fact is, to-day, that Parliament, which should be the pacemaker, which should be giving the lead in individual initiatives, which should be bursting with dynamic energies, has never been more devoid of just those qualities that are needed for these purposes. 'We have too much domination by the Front Benches', declared my old friend, John Jennings,* in the debate on the Business of Parliament immediately subsequent to the 1966 General Election: but he is 'the last of the Mohicans'. The reasons for this are plain: the sanctions exerted by the Party machines against such troublesome

* John Jennings, Conservative M.P. for Burton-on-Trent.

attributes have never been more severe, nor exercised in more irresponsible fashion.

It is often said, half-jestingly, that M.P.s are robots. But it is the triumph of the Chairman of the Carlisle Conservative Association in 1963 to have proved this statement beyond a peradventure in as much as he dragooned the entire Conservative Party to endorse his audacious claims. Let us repeat his words:

'Dr. Johnson has always been an outspoken M.P. and within reason there is no objection to this. *But it is of course an Association's duty to decide in this context what is reasonable and what is not.*'

The meaning of these words is quite clear. Behind every Conservative M.P. there sits his puppet-master, the Chairman of his Association, pulling the strings in armchair comfort, not so much telling him what to say, but even more important, telling him what he should not say.

Since no steps have been taken to repudiate this, this is clearly the situation in the Conservative Party. If so, 'The Great Divide', as far as political freedom is concerned, is not between the two Parties, but between those who stand for a slave Parliament and those who stand for a free one. Until we have this latter I can foresee little hope of the national revival for which we yearn.

APPENDIX I

Letter from Dr. Donald Johnson to the Chairman of the
Carlisle Conservative Association written on 14th October 1963
and read to the Meeting of the Executive the following evening.

The Chairman,
Carlisle Conservative Association,
2 Chatsworth Square,
Carlisle.

Dear Chairman,

Even though it has been superseded to some extent by events,
I can see no reason for substantial alteration to the message which
I sent you ten days ago before I left for the Continent. However,
I am sure that you will wish me to add further comments in the
new circumstances of the Prime Minister's resignation and, whereas
I will understand that you will wish only to give a précis of my
former message, I would much appreciate it if you would convey
this one in full to the members of the Executive who are meeting
tonight.

I hope that it will now be clear that the attitude I have recently
taken was not based on any personal animosity towards Mr.
Macmillan so much as on my opinion that he was a sick man
who had no apparent appreciation of the seriousness of his own
condition. It is now revealed that he has been under medical
attention for some while and a moment's thought will demonstrate
that the present accident to his health could have occurred at an
even more disastrous time to the Party than the present one.

It is, of course, something of an advantage to be a doctor on
such occasions. However, from my point of view it is the more
distressing to think that this is yet another instance, in addition to
others which I have retailed, of what I can justly claim to have
been wise counsel based on experience being brushed aside.

It is well known also that a large number of my Parliamentary colleagues shared my views and that these, too, were equally disregarded.

It is as a result of this that our affairs at the present juncture are in the melting pot. Indeed, so much is this so that I can scarcely be expected to give a definite answer at this moment to the question which tonight's meeting will naturally wish to pose to me concerning my intentions for the General Election.

I can, however, give some indication of my attitude. It is that, consequent on recent events, I have the very gravest concern in regard to the present position and status of the back-bench Member of Parliament: so much is this so that I cannot pledge my support for any of the present active contenders for the succession, until such time as I can receive the assurances which I feel that I need on this score and an answer to a number of pertinent questions that come into my mind.

I have greatly appreciated the courtesy and understanding of the Carlisle Association in consenting to the recent standstill while the issue has worked itself out thus far: and I hope accordingly that I may ask their discretion for a while longer for this specific purpose. In the meantime I would be pleased to make an early appointment to meet the officers with a view to putting forward a more detailed statement and subsequently keeping in touch with them until the issue is determined.

To prevent misunderstanding, however, may I make it clear that I am not hereby sacrificing my liberty to ventilate my opinions in public statements. Indeed it is my view that public curiosity is now focused on us to such an extent that it will be necessary for me to issue a suitable précis of this statement to the Press.

Yours sincerely,
(Signed) Donald McI. Johnson.

APPENDIX II

Letter to the Editor, *Cumberland News*, Friday, 18th September, 1964.

'OUR ACTION JUSTIFIED,' says Tory President

Now that Dr. Johnson has announced that he is going to stand in Carlisle at the General Election as an independent candidate, we on behalf of the Carlisle Conservative Association, consider that it is necessary to restate the reasons why we felt unable to re-adopt Dr. Johnson as the official Conservative candidate.

Since 1959 when he was re-elected, Dr. Johnson many times complained to the Officers of the Association about his dissatisfaction with his lot in Parliament, continually expressed doubts as to his willingness to stand again at the next election, and even when a year ago the Association felt the adoption of a prospective candidate could be delayed no longer, Dr. Johnson still refused to give a firm assurance that he would stand, if asked.

Impression

He gave the Association the impression that he considered the Prime Minister and the leaders of the party were failing to appreciate his peculiar talents and qualifications and to accord him his proper place in their counsels.

In 1963 Dr. Johnson showed himself highly critical of Mr. Macmillan's leadership and said so very loudly in public. He emphasised his attitude by choosing to be absent from the House of Commons during the debate on the Profumo case—a debate vital to the interests of the Conservative Government—and ensuring maximum publicity by having himself photographed by the Press playing golf.

The Association has never questioned the right of Dr. Johnson or any other M.P. to criticise the leadership or the policies of the party, but many members felt strongly that a loyal Conservative would have confined himself to protesting as strongly as possible through the adequate party channels, and would not have sought to gain personal publicity and advantage at the expense of the party's interests.

Disagreement

The disagreement with the Association came to a head when Dr. Johnson told us, following the resignation of Mr. Macmillan, that he would not pledge his support to any new leader of the party, whoever he might be, unless he, the leader, agreed to fulfil certain conditions which Dr. Johnson would lay down.

The Officers felt that once again Dr. Johnson was attempting to reap personal advantage from party difficulties, and they informed him that they intended to put the whole question to the Executive Council.

Dr. Johnson had already addressed the Executive Council to give his views, and he agreed it would be better for him not to be present at the meeting on October 14, 1963.

Overwhelmingly

At that meeting the Executive showed itself overwhelmingly against Dr. Johnson's attitude and passed a motion of no confidence in him. It also decided to proceed with the selection of a new candidate.

Dr. Johnson then refused to accept the decision of the properly constituted Executive of the Association, claiming that he had not been allowed to put his case and inspired a requisition for a special general meeting.

The special general meeting was held on December 30, 1963, and was fully reported at the time in the Press. Suffice to say that the meeting decisively confirmed the action of the Executive. Dr. Johnson thanked the President of the Association for his fair conduct of the meeting, and said 'I accept the decision, as I said I would.'*

* The only decision I said that I would accept was that in regard to retaining my seat until the end of Parliament. D.J.

Campaign

It appears, however, that Dr. Johnson had second thoughts, and almost immediately launched a campaign in the Press of diatribes against the Association and its Officers, past and present.

He claimed that the special general meeting was not representative of the Association, and was not competent to decide not to re-adopt him, though he had himself demanded it.

Dr. Johnson's conduct since the meeting in December has convinced the Association that our action was right and justified—Yours, etc.

President,
Chairman,

Carlisle Conservative Association.

INDEX

(*Author's Note: An index in a book of this kind presents certain difficulties owing to the continual transition of the political scene and its personalities. The factors involved in the case of M.P.s include, of course, the natural claims of mortality, retirement from the House, defeat at Elections and translation to other appointments and to the House of Lords. Thus I have thought it desirable to designate by this title all those who have been M.P.s during the span of thirty years covered by this book, but I have put this designation in brackets in the case of all those no longer in the House at the time of writing. I have applied the same criterion to those who unfortunately have to be designated 'the late'.*)

A

B

H

I

J